Books by Millicent Selsam

Stars, Mosquitoes & Crocodiles: The American Travels of Alexander Von Humboldt
Biography of an Atom (with J. Bronowski)
Vegetables from Stems & Leaves
Tomato and Other Fruit Vegetables
Bulbs, Corms & Such
The Harlequin Moth: Its Life Story
Seeds & More Seeds

The Don't Throw It, Grow It
Book of Houseplants

The Don't Throw It, Grow It Book of Houseplants

Millicent Selsam
and Deborah Peterson

Illustrated by Grambs Miller

Random House   New York

Library of Congress Cataloging in Publication Data
Selsam, Millicent Ellis, 1912–
The don't throw it, grow it book of houseplants.
1. House plants.   I. Peterson, Deborah, joint author.   II. Title.
SB419.S399   635.9'65   76–53494
ISBN 0–394–41076–9
ISBN 0–394–73308–8 pbk.

Manufactured in the United States of America
9 8 7 6 5 4 3 2
First Edition

To Hart Peterson

Contents

Introduction

This book began when I attended a lecture at a meeting of the Indoor Light Gardening Society in New York. The title of the lecture was "Eat the Fruit, Plant the Seed." Deborah Peterson, the lecturer, displayed a trayful of luscious tropical fruit and then showed slides illustrating the results if you planted the pits or seeds of the various fruits. I was intrigued. For years I had been planting various vegetables and fruits in my own "kitchen garden."

After the lecture I asked Deborah Peterson if she would like to do a book with me on "how to grow everything but the kitchen sink." She looked a little dubious, so I left her my name, address and telephone number, and departed. The next morning Debbie Peterson called. It seemed she had checked me out with the head of the Indoor Light Gardening Society and found that I was "legitimate."

And so began this adventure. We have found that we share a love of people, food and plants and enjoy scouting around for exotic plants to grow. We started with the vegetables and fruits one ordinarily has in the kitchen. Then we found the world of the Middle East, Latin America and the Orient in stores within easy traveling distance of our homes. (We live in New York City, where there are lots of ethnic stores, but don't underestimate your own city. Marvelous markets exist all over this diverse country.)

It's a long wait from spring to spring, and if you have the planting craze and can't wait for the usual seeds of vegetables and flowers, you can have a wonderful time in your own apartment or home planting anything that can possibly grow. If you have a pit in your mouth and don't know what to do with it, plant it. If a potato is growing in your bag of potatoes, plant it. If you can't bear to throw out an avocado pit, plant it.

In our kitchens right now we have sweet-potato vines climbing up the window, beans, peas, lentils and peanuts sprouting in pie plates, casseroles boasting lush turnips, beets, radishes, kohlrabi and Jerusalem artichokes, and a row of fig trees growing in a plastic box. In big bowls on our tables we collect the fruits available in the market each week. It's not so much that we love to eat the fruit but that there are seeds inside all those fruits that can grow into plants.

If you have never grown anything before, you have a delightful time ahead. Even if you are an experienced grower of houseplants, this book will open new doors for you. There are an incredible number of plants you can enjoy by planting the common vegetables and fruits that you have in the kitchen. And once you start combing the Latin American markets and Chinese, Japanese and Italian grocery stores for new plants to grow, you are hooked on a wonderful pastime.

We have tried everything, but in this book we will leave out our failures and tell you how to grow only the plants with which we have succeeded. So make room on your window-sill, or plant table or wherever you'd like to display unusually interesting plants.

If this book has any message at all, it is that growing is easy, fun, and there are lots of ways to do it. Even the experts don't follow every direction or suggestion.

Start with a few seeds or tubers and soon you will get the feel of it. Before long you will want to plant more and more, and that's when the fun begins.

1
The Nitty-Gritty of Growing

T his book will show you how to grow lovely house-plants from the pits, seeds, tubers, roots and vegetable tops that are either ordinarily discarded or used as staples in your kitchen. We also hope that you will be inspired to seek out the more exotic fruits and vegetables for planting.

If you've never grown plants before or need to catch up on some basics, here are some fundamental facts about growing. There is no such thing as a "green thumb." Plants grow well if you have a knowledge of the conditions they require and if you are interested enough to supply them. What follows are the basic growing requirements of plants.

Containers

The first question that comes up is, What am I going to plant in? Of course, there are the usual flower pots—clay or plastic. But you can also use plastic kitchen containers or plastic glasses. Large rectangular plastic containers about three inches high, used to store cold cuts or cheese, can hold many rows of seeds. A plastic bread box is great if you need lots of room.

If you use a plastic container, make some holes in the bottom so that excess water will drain off. To do this, simply heat a small skewer in the gas flame or on the heating coil of the electric stove until it is hot, then push it through the bottom of the plastic container. The skewer stays hot enough to make several holes at one time. Aluminum-foil pie and cake pans work well, too, if you punch holes in the bottom of those that do not already have them.

There is also something new on the market called Jiffy pellets or One-steps. Essentially they are flat disks of compressed peat moss with a netting around them. They combine the function of a pot and potting soil. When dry, they look

like small dark cookies, but if you wet them they expand into miniature flower pots into which you can pop a seed "in a jiffy." Use a quarter of a cup of water per Jiffy pellet, and wait five minutes till all the water is soaked up. The Jiffy pellets are somewhat expensive (about ten cents each), but they make life simple for the grower with a pit in his or her mouth. The peat moss is sterile, so that it contains no weeds or pests. All you need do is press a seed into it. If the seed is large you may have to take out some of the peat, plant the seed, and cover it again. Keep the Jiffy pellets in a container just big enough to hold them. Add water if they seem to be drying out. You can prevent drying, however, by pulling a plastic bag over the container.

When the plant is tall enough to be moved, just plant Jiffy pellet and all in a bigger pot. This eliminates transplant shock, which occurs when the roots of a young plant are dug up to be moved to a larger pot.

Soil

In the "old days" you were told to go out and dig up some soil in the garden for planting your seeds. Today, when hardly anyone has soil of his or her own, especially in the city, it is a good idea to use the sterilized media you can buy in a five-and-ten or at a florist's. There are many kinds of sterile growing media:

Vermiculite is exploded mica; the layers of mica separate when heated, and each layer can then hold a film of water. It does not pack down and therefore holds air between the pieces of mica. Air around the roots is absolutely necessary to prevent their "drowning."

Perlite looks like coarse white sand. It is formed when obsidian, a glassy volcanic rock, is heated. Like vermiculite, it holds lots of water and does not pack down, leaving plenty of air between the grains. When you open a bag of perlite, spray lightly with water to avoid the dust that comes up when you handle it.

Peat moss is the partially rotted remains of sphagnum

moss which is found in bogs and swamps. It, too, holds water well and does not pack down.

Any of these sterile media is good for planting seeds. But the best growing medium for seeds is a mixture of one-third vermiculite, one-third perlite and one-third peat moss. This makes a light, airy *soilless mix*. For established plants the soilless mix has the disadvantage of being very light in weight. Large plants require a heavier soil to hold them in place.

In the five-and-ten you can find other sterile media, such as potting soil, African violet soil and humus. Potting soil is sterilized garden soil. African violet soil is potting soil plus a good proportion of peat. Humus is organic matter usually made of either decomposed leaves or peat.

To make a heavier soil mix, use two parts of potting soil, one part peat or humus and one part of either vermiculite or perlite. This makes a good general *average soil mix*.

Whatever mix you use, the soil should be evenly moist before planting. Add water slowly and mix thoroughly. To test for adequate moisture, take a handful and gently squeeze it. The soil should stick together but crumble easily in your hands. If there is too much water, add additional soil mix.

Fertilizer

There are no minerals available from perlite and vermiculite. Peat moss has some, but not many. Therefore, if you use a soilless mix, you should water your plants with liquid fertilizer (available in many stores) every two weeks.

If you use the average soil mix, the potting soil in the mix will supply minerals for about a month or two. After that you will have to fertilize regularly. Be sure to follow the directions on the bottle or box. Don't get carried away. You can easily burn the roots and kill a plant by overfertilizing. Also, do not fertilize if the plant seems to be in a resting stage, which usually occurs in the winter when the days are short and the sunshine not very bright. Fertilize when the plant seems to be growing actively, putting out new shoots and leaves and buds.

Many people are surprised to learn that plants have to be fed. Plants do have a unique ability to make their own food. They can manufacture sugars and starches from carbon dioxide and water, but they cannot manufacture proteins necessary for growth unless there are certain chemical elements dissolved in the water of the soil in which they are growing. The most important of these elements are nitrogen, phosphorus and potassium. Nitrogen makes leaves and stems grow and stay green. Phosphorus encourages flower, fruit and seed. Potassium stiffens stems and promotes sturdy, compact growth. Any liquid fertilizer you buy has these three elements in it as well as many other trace elements such as magnesium, boron and iron. These trace elements are needed only in very tiny amounts, but plants cannot do without them.

Germination of Large Tubers and Large Seeds Using a Peat Moss Bag

The peat moss bag is a simple device which has turned out to be one of the most useful and successful secrets of germination. To make it, fill a plastic bag half full with peat moss.

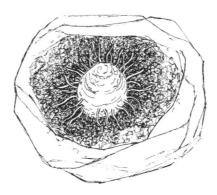

Moisten the peat to the consistency of a flaky piecrust. Squeeze out any excess moisture; if the peat is too wet it can cause rot.

Originally we used the peat bag for tubers whose tops and bottoms we could not determine, i.e., ginger, ñame, malanga and Jerusalem artichokes. We placed some moist peat in the bag, added our tubers and covered them with more moist peat. Then we closed the bag by folding the top over and placed it in a warm dark spot. In a short time the buds sprouted on the top and roots grew from the bottom. Germination was very rapid. A Jerusalem artichoke started in a regular pot ordinarily takes from two to three weeks, whereas one started in the peat bag sprouted within a matter of days.

One day we found ourselves stuck with some twenty avocado pits. No true grower can let a seed go to waste and we are no exception, but we had neither the time nor energy nor enough toothpicks or glasses to plant twenty pits. The peat bag seemed the easiest way out. It provided the pits with the moist, womblike atmosphere of the mother fruit and gave us a little time to get around to them. We forgot about them completely until some three weeks later, when we noticed a tangle of roots and stems protruding through the forgotten bag. Both the root and stem development were much thicker and sturdier than on those plants we had started in either soil or water.

Several weeks later we found ourselves with several dozen large seeds about one inch long. Previously we had potted large seeds in individual pots, but this time we put the seeds in the peat bag. Three weeks later the bag looked like a tangle of worms, with roots and stems all over the place— each seed had sprouted and developed a strong root system. Detecting the germination of small seeds in a peat bag is like looking for a needle in a haystack, but large seeds sprout extremely well in this medium.

Germination of Small Seeds

To plant small seeds, put moist soilless mix into a container to within an inch of the top. Then scatter the seeds on the surface and cover with more moist soilless mix. Usually you should cover the seed with twice as much soil as the seed is thick: A quarter-inch seed should be covered with one half inch of soil. Press tiny dustlike seeds into the soil with your fingers. Slip a plastic bag over the seed container and put it in a warm place. (Most seeds do not need light to germinate.)

When you see germination starting, put the container in the brightest place you have available. A sunny windowsill is best. If you have fluorescent light, place the container two inches beneath the lamps. When the seedlings are an inch high, remove the plastic bag. Keep the pot evenly moist at all times.

Use sterile soil mix to prevent "damping off," a fungus disease that attacks and rots young seedlings where they emerge from the soil. If damping off occurs, remove all diseased seedlings as soon as you see them. Do not use this soil again.

Bottom Heat to Aid Germination

Many seeds, tubers and roots come from tropical countries. They will sprout faster if they are supplied with bottom heat. They can be put on a radiator, with a few layers of newspaper or cardboard on the metal to keep the pots from getting too much heat. Or you can put the pots on an electric tray used to keep food warm and set the dial for low heat. The temperature of the soil should be about 80 degrees. When the plants sprout, remove them from the bottom heat.

Stratification of Seeds to Aid Germination

Seeds from fruits of northern and temperate climates require a cold period before they can germinate. The process of exposing the seeds to cold is called stratification, which mimics winter in the plants' original habitat and breaks the seeds' dormancy.

To stratify, fill half a plastic container (cottage cheese dish or the like) with moistened peat moss, scatter the seeds on the moss, cover the container, and place it in the refrigerator.

Check weekly to be sure the peat is still moist. After six to eight weeks remove the container and place it in a warm spot in the house. Keep the plastic bag over it. Germination will take place within three weeks.

Among seeds which benefit from this cold treatment are chestnuts, almonds, apples, pears, peaches, grapes and kiwi.

Transplanting

Your plants should be kept in pots just big enough to let them grow until the roots fill the pot. A simple rule of thumb is to use a pot one inch wider than the crown of the plant, or if it is a tuber, one inch wider than the tuber. If pots are too big you can easily overwater, literally drowning the plant because the roots die from lack of oxygen. Whatever size the pot, there is much less danger of overwatering if you use a loose soil mix.

When a plant grows too big for its pot, it has to be moved. Otherwise the roots will produce a tight mass that prevents them from functioning. If you find yourself having to water every day, it is time to examine the roots.

To see if a plant needs repotting, water it first, then holding the stem between your fingers, turn the pot upside

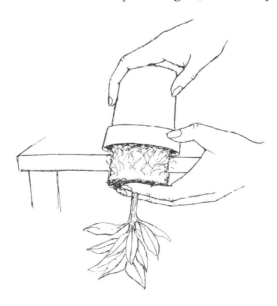

down. Now rap the rim against a hard surface. The whole ball of earth in the pot will slide forward. If the roots completely fill the ball of earth so that no soil can be removed from the surface, it is time to repot. Use a pot just about one inch larger than the old one. If it is a clay pot with one large hole at the bottom, place a few pieces of broken clay pot—called "crock"—over the hole, add an inch of soil mix and set the plant on it. Most plastic pots have small holes and do not require "crocking." An inch of soil mix may be poured directly in the bottom of the pot and the plant placed on it. Fill the area around the plant with fresh mix, then rap the pot to settle the soil around the roots. Press down around the stem with your fingers. Add more mix, if needed, to bring the soil level within an inch of the rim of the pot—this leaves plenty of room for watering.

Light

Plants need light to manufacture food. They do this in a process called photosynthesis: using the energy of sunlight, carbon dioxide and water are combined by the plant cells to form sugars and starches. The plant uses these sugars and starches to grow.

Plants differ in their light requirements. If your plant turns pale green and the stems become very long, giving the plant a leggy appearance, it needs more light. If the plant is getting more light than it needs, the leaves may be scorched. Too much light in indoor gardening is rarely a problem.

Plants keep bending their leaves toward the light to get the greatest amount of light energy for the manufacturing process. So in order to avoid a lopsided look you should turn them frequently.

Many plants will do well under artificial light provided by fluorescent lamps. The standard commercial lamps, ordinary daylight, cool white and warm white fluorescent tubes can be used. There are also special "growth" tubes, such as Sylvania's Gro-Lux and Duro-Test's Vita-Lite. They are more expensive and usually not necessary for the ordinary plant.

To approximate natural light, it is a good idea to mix several different kinds of fluorescent tubes because they give off different wavelengths of light.

Sunlight is made up of several colors which you can see only if the light passes through a prism, or is broken up, as by raindrops in a rainbow. Then you can see that white light is actually made up of a spectrum, or series of colors, that starts with short violet rays at one end and goes from blue to green to yellow to orange to red. Beyond this spectrum there are rays we can't see—ultraviolet, which is shorter than violet, and infrared, which is longer than the red rays.

Which of these rays do the plants use? Perhaps all of them are important to plant growth. But photosynthesis takes place mostly in the blue and red parts of the spectrum. The light of fluorescent bulbs gives off red and blue rays as well as other colors, and so is suitable for plant growth. The average Mazda electric light bulb gives off too much heat and is weak in the blue part of the spectrum.

Water

Without water, a plant becomes limp and wilts. With too much water, the roots are deprived of air, which they need to keep from decaying. The trick is to keep the soil moist but . Ot too wet.

It is impossible to give general rules for all plants, but you can start by watering your plants only when the top soil feels dry. Do not sprinkle a little water on top and leave it at that. Water thoroughly—add water until it seeps out through the hole in the bottom of the pot or container. Then don't water until the top soil feels dry again. It is best to use water that is slightly warm. Mix the water from the cold and hot water taps until it feels tepid.

Water enters the roots and goes up through the stems and leaves; then it evaporates through pores in the leaves. It is this evaporation that keeps pulling more water up from the roots. The amount of water a plant evaporates will depend on whether the leaves are thin or thick. Plants with large thin leaves lose water rapidly, so the soil in which these plants grow must not be allowed to get completely dry. Plants with thicker leaves, such as philodendron, will lose much less water by evaporation. And, or course, cacti, with thick stems and no leaves, do not lose water easily and can be allowed to dry out between waterings.

Plants kept in a cool, moist place will dry out more slowly than plants kept in a warm, dry place. Plants in smaller pots dry out faster than plants in large containers.

Another factor to watch out for is the stage of growth of a plant. If a plant is actively growing and putting out new leaves and stems and flowers, it needs more water than a plant that appears to have stopped growing. Many plants go through a rest period in winter, at which time they need much less water than they do in the spring, when active growth begins.

Humidity

Most houseplants come from warm, moist climates, but the average house or apartment where they are to grow is as dry as a desert when the heat is on. To increase the amount of moisture in the air, you can do several things. You can group your plants. Keeping them together does some good because each plant gives off water vapor and makes the air above it more moist. But the more effective thing to do is to group plants on shallow trays filled with pebbles: add water up to the top layer of pebbles and keep the water at that level at all times. Evaporation from the water in the trays will add lots of moisture to the air because of the extent of the trays' surface

area. (Water in deep containers hung on radiators does very little good.) Spraying the leaves of plants with water from a sprayer with a fine-mist nozzle helps a lot, too.

You can also buy a humidifier, which will keep the air in your apartment beneficial for both plants and yourself.

Insect Pests

Examine your plants regularly to locate insect pests:

Plant lice usually cluster at the tips of young growing shoots.

Masses of white cottony tufts in the axils (the angles between the stems and the leaf stalks) of branches and on other parts of the stems and leaves are a sign of mealybugs.

Scale insects are tiny, shiny oval lumps on stems and leaves.

White flies are generally found on the undersides of leaves and fly off when disturbed.

Mites are too tiny to see, but you can find their fine webs on the undersides of leaves.

The best way to keep these common insects from at-tacking your plants is to wash your plants regularly with plain lukewarm water. If the infestation is bad, use soapy water made with brown soap. Repeat the washing every few days for several weeks because new eggs will keep hatching.

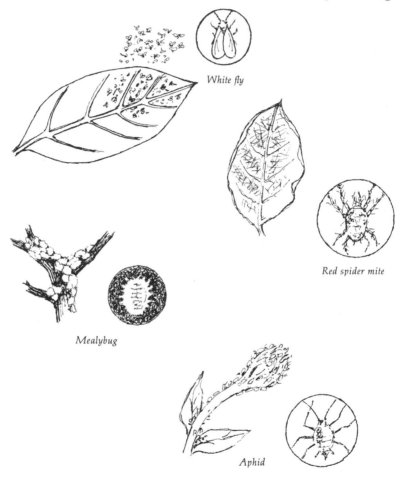

White fly

Red spider mite

Mealybug

Aphid

Mealybugs and scale can be removed by using alcohol on a Q-Tip or on a paintbrush. After removing those you can see, use the alcohol to carefully clean all the rest of the leaves and stems.

If you cannot control the insect problem by these methods, you can use a houseplant spray. However, many of these are poisonous and should be used with caution. Select sprays made with pyrethrum, rotenone or malathion.

The best cure is prophylactic. A sterile growing medium, clean pots, well-scrubbed tubers, pits and seeds, plenty of ventilation and no overcrowding will usually do the trick.

2

Plants from Kitchen Vegetables

Ever since we began growing beets and turnips we cannot think of them as just vegetables. They are now house plants as well, and when we shop for them we are not only buying tonight's dinner, but preparing a centerpiece for the table.

There are surprises in store when you grow plants from vegetables. Turnips and radishes actually bloom. Sweet potatoes have small purple flowers like morning glories. White potatoes have crinkly leaves and lovely flowers shading from white to purple.

Beans make pretty plants, with flowers like sweet peas, and they have added attractions: The leaves close up at night and in their early germinating stages are delicious to eat as sprouts.

Chickpeas make charming hanging-basket plants. Lentils have dainty foliage. Squash plants have amazingly big yellow flowers, and although the plants will last only a few months, they are attractive and should not be missed. The descriptions and directions that follow will lead you to your own discoveries. Enjoy them!

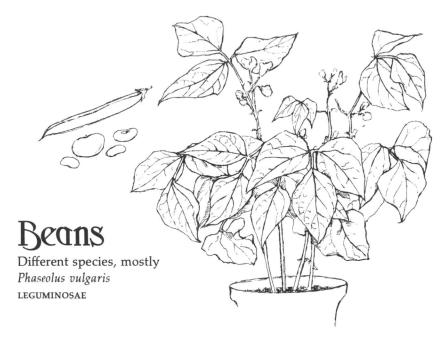

Beans

Different species, mostly
Phaseolus vulgaris
LEGUMINOSAE

Origin. Western Hemisphere. When explorers came to America, they found the Indians eating hundreds of different kinds of beans. Lima beans, white navy beans, black beans, pinto beans, string beans and many other kinds were being used all over North, South and Central America. Practically every tribe had its own special kind of beans. Soon these new varieties spread all over the world.

How to Grow. If you are using dried beans, rinse in a colander and soak them overnight. If fresh beans are used, plant immediately.

To plant: Fill two thirds of a four-inch pot with soilless mix, tamping the mix down to settle the soil and remove large air pockets. Place three beans on the soil about an inch apart and cover with a half inch of soil. Keep the soil constantly damp, not wet, until the beans sprout. Beans sprout in a matter of days. As the plants grow, pull out the smaller specimens and allow one good-sized plant to grow. Keep the pot on a sunny windowsill and water well. The bean plant can flower and produce new edible pods in about eight weeks.

Habit of Growth. Pole beans are vines. The majority of beans are short bushy plants about one foot high. They have leaves divided into three parts. The pastel-colored flowers appear within a few weeks. Self-pollination takes place and seed pods will form. If you let these mature, you can plant your own home-grown seeds.

If you look at your bean plant at night, you might think it is drooping. What is really happening is that the leaves close up at night. It is a good example of the power of movement in plants.

Beans as Sprouts

Beans are among the easiest and most delicious seeds to sprout. Bean sprouts have been used in Oriental cooking for centuries, but it is only recently that Americans have discovered their unique flavor.

Kidney beans, lima beans, navy beans, pinto beans, soybeans and mung beans (available in Oriental groceries) can all be sprouted.

To sprout the beans, take one quarter of a cup of dried beans and rinse them to wash off dust and dirt. Then soak them overnight using about four times as much lukewarm water as beans. In the morning, rinse the beans in a strainer, and spread them thinly over the bottom of a container large enough so that they can be scattered over the surface without crowding. Use a plastic or china dish, a glass pie plate, or an enamel pot. Lay wet paper towels over the beans, cover with another dish and set in a warm place. Check at night to make sure the paper is wet.

The next day, rinse the beans in a strainer and spread them out on the dish again. Moisten more paper towels and cover the dish. Repeat the rinsing of the seeds every day. (The large beans will sprout better if they are rinsed twice a day.)

Soybean and mung bean sprouts are ready to be used

when they are two to three inches long. They will reach this size in four to five days. Other large beans should be harvested when they are about one inch long (this takes about three days).

Mung beans can be used raw, but the large beans should be shelled and cooked for a few minutes before they are eaten.

Bean sprouts are rich in many vitamins and minerals and give you the pleasure of seeing real food grow in a matter of days.

Beet

Beta vulgaris
CHENOPODIACEAE

Origin. The ancestor of the beet is a sprawling seaside plant—the sea beet—that still grows along the Mediterranean coasts of southern Europe. It has a tough, woody, slender root not at all like the tender beet root which has been cultivated from it over the course of many years.

How to Grow. Buy only firm fresh beet roots that have tiny new leaves sprouting at the top.

Our favorite way to grow beets is in a pebble tray, an attractive soup bowl or serving dish. Place the beets on a one-inch layer of pebbles, sprout side up, and add more pebbles to hold the beets in place. (Pebbles may be bought in any five-and-ten in the pet or plant section.) Leave at least two thirds of each beet exposed. Add water to the level of the pebbles and make sure this water level is always maintained.

Habit of Growth. Within five days, stunning dark-green foliage with thick red stems and veins will emerge from the tops. The leaves reach a length of six to eight inches. (Once the leaves have emerged, we use this dish garden as a centerpiece for the table.) The foliage will die down in about two or three weeks. Don't throw the beets out. If you are lucky, and we have been many times, the beets will shoot up a compact flower stalk of pale-purple blooms.

Beets are biennials, which means it takes two years from

seed to bloom. The roots you buy in the store formed underground the first year; if left in the ground, the second year, the beet roots will bear flowers and seeds. What you do when you plant a beet root is "jump the gun" on its natural development.

Carrot

Daucus carota
UMBELLIFERAE

Origin. Central Asia. The ancient Greeks believed carrots to be an aphrodisiac. By the first century the plant was being cultivated for medicinal purposes, as a tonic, as a poultice and for snakebite.

How to Grow. Cut off the top two inches of several carrots. Select an attractive bowl and put a one-inch layer of pebbles in it. Place the carrot tops on the pebbles cut side down, and add more pebbles to hold them in place. Leave at least one half inch of the carrot exposed. Add water to the level of the pebbles and maintain this water level at all times. Keep the dish garden in bright light.

You can also plant the whole root in soil in a flower pot. In six to eight weeks the plant will send up a stalk with flowers that resemble Queen Anne's lace.

Habit of Growth. Carrots make a charming dish garden because of the lovely feathery green leaves that grow out of the tops. Carrot dish gardens are short-lived (three to six weeks), but since they are so easy to grow, you can keep carrot tops sprouting as frequently as you use carrots in preparing meals.

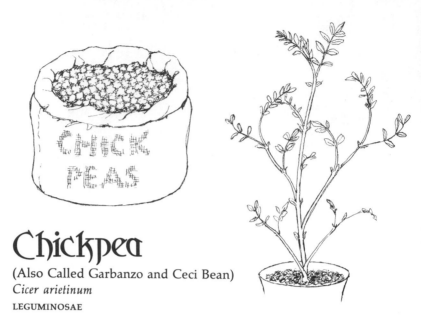

Chickpea

(Also Called Garbanzo and Ceci Bean)
Cicer arietinum
LEGUMINOSAE

Origin. Europe and Central Asia. The exact origin of the chickpea is buried in antiquity. The plant grows wild throughout Europe and Central Asia and may well have been one of the staples of early man. Egyptians, Hebrews and Greeks are known to have grown it, and today chickpeas are cultivated throughout the tropical and subtropical parts of the world.

How to Grow. Fill two thirds of a four-inch pot with moist soilless mix. Place three chickpeas on the soil and cover with another half inch of soil. Cover the container with a plastic bag or a piece of sheet plastic. The seeds will germinate within a few days. When the sprouts appear, remove the plastic and put the container in a sunny place.

Habit of Growth. Feathery green leaves trail over the edges of the pot and make a charming hanging basket indoors. The plants need full sun, warmth and lots of water to produce flowers and fruit. This plant is an annual and begins to die after about six months.

Jerusalem Artichoke

Helianthus tuberosus
COMPOSITAE

Origin. North America. The Jerusalem artichoke neither came from Jerusalem nor is it an artichoke. It probably developed from a species of sunflower that is found in the Mississippi Valley. When Champlain arrived at Cape Cod in 1605, he found the plant being used as food by the Indians. Although it did not reach Europe until the early part of the seventeenth century, it is now grown throughout the Northern Hemisphere.

How to Grow. Jerusalem artichokes are tubers which look like bumpy potatoes. They are round with little nubs and a smooth light-brown skin. Put a whole tuber in a bag of moist peat moss and keep the bag in a warm place. It will germinate rapidly, and within a week top buds will begin to swell and thick roots will develop. Because this is an exceptionally large plant, select a pot some three inches larger than the tuber. When the roots are three inches long and the buds clearly swollen, plant the tuber horizontally in average soil mix (see p. 5). Do not cover completely with soil, but allow the buds to show just above the surface.

Habit of Growth. The Jerusalem artichoke is a fast-growing plant which can attain a height of three to five feet. One tuber can yield as many as fifteen stems. The leaves, some three inches long, are soft and fuzzy green. The plant will bloom if placed in a cool southern window or a terrace garden in the spring. (The flowers will look like small yellow sunflowers.) The foliage will die back in a few months, but underground there will be new tubers that are smaller than the ones sold commercially. Instead of using these new tubers, you should plant the supermarket variety if you want large plants.

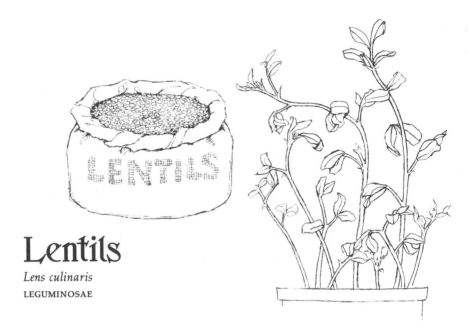

Lentils

Lens culinaris
LEGUMINOSAE

Origin. Asia. Lentils have been found in prehistoric sites in Asia and Europe and in Egyptian tombs over four thousand years old. Egyptians apparently believed that lentils increased mental powers; the Romans believed exactly the opposite. Today lentils are a staple throughout the world.

How to Grow. Fill a four-inch pot two thirds full with moist average soil mix (see p. 5). Place a half-dozen lentils on the soil and cover with a quarter of an inch of moist soil. Place the pots in a brightly lit window and keep the soil moist. The seeds will sprout within a few days.

Habit of Growth. A pot of lentils a foot tall makes a pretty sight, with delicate gray-green leaves and small bluish flowers. Though the plant will last only a few months, it is well worth growing because it is both charming and inexpensive.

Onion, Garlic and Shallots

Allium species
LILIACEAE

Origin. The onion family has been known from the dawn of history. The Egyptians saw the onion as a model of the universe because they thought the spheres of hell, earth and heaven were also in concentric rings. Garlic has always been thought to be good for various illnesses, and claims are still made for its value as an aid to digestion and in reducing high blood pressure and relieving bronchitis. Onions contain a substance called allylaldehyde, which is antiseptic and can destroy certain bacteria.

How to Grow. Select an attractive bowl or serving dish about three to four inches high (a Chinese soup bowl does nicely). Put a two-inch layer of pebbles at the bottom of the dish, some onions, garlic cloves, and shallot bulbs flat end down on the pebbles and add water to the point where it covers the bottom of the bulbs. Keep the water at this level and leave the dish in a bright place so that the stems will turn green.

To produce your own garlic or shallots to use in cooking, break up the bulbs into individual cloves and plant them in average soil mix (see p. 5) about one inch deep and five inches apart. Put the container or pot in a sunny place and fertilize every two weeks. Each clove will produce a whole bulb with many cloves.

Habit of Growth. Roots come out of the bottom of the bulb; the bud inside the bulb or clove grows out into long green leaves. If you use this dish garden as a dining-room centerpiece, your guests can snip off the green leaves and learn the subtle taste differences between the shoots of onion, garlic and shallots.

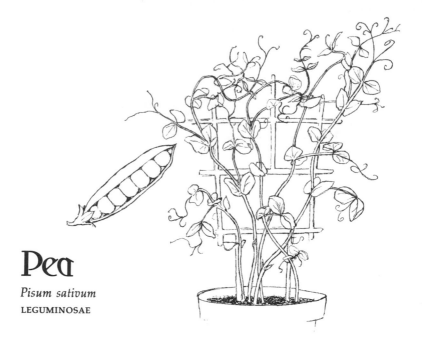

Pea

Pisum sativum
LEGUMINOSAE

Origin. Europe. Peas have been found in five-thousand-year-old dwellings in the lake region of Switzerland. From there they spread southward to Sumer (today the part of Iraq near the Persian Gulf) and then to Egypt.

The ancients probably used them dried. Meat was heavily salted to preserve it, and cooking with dried peas helped to draw out the salt or at least to distribute the taste.

Fresh peas were the rage in Europe about the time that Catherine de Medici became queen of France. In 1669 Madame de Maintenon described the passion for peas as a kind of madness: "The anxiety to eat them, the pleasure of having eaten them, and the desire to eat them again, are the three great matters which have been discussed by our princes for four days past."

Their popularity rapidly spread to the English court and to the American colonies. Today they are cultivated in all countries with a temperate climate.

How to Grow. Open a fresh peapod and remove the seeds, or use dried peas that have been soaked overnight. Fill a four-inch pot two thirds full with moist soilless mix. Place three peas on the surface and cover with an inch of the mix. Place the pot in a sunny window, and water when the soil dries out. Use liquid fertilizer every two weeks.

Habit of Growth. The peas sprout in a week and develop into vines which climb by means of tendrils and need to be supported. The plants will flower and bear fruit if grown in a cool, sunny place. Pea flowers are self-pollinating, so you can actually grow peas indoors.

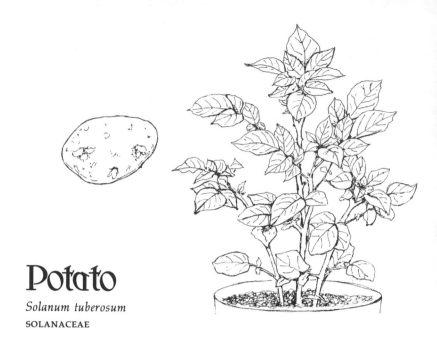

Potato

Solanum tuberosum
SOLANACEAE

Origin. South America. The potato was brought from South America to Europe by Spanish sailing ships and was introduced in North America by European settlers in the early seventeenth century.

How to Grow. Pick a small potato with buds already starting to sprout. Fill one third of a six-inch pot with moist average soil mix (see p. 5); put the potato on it, and cover with an inch of soil. Keep it in bright sun, and water when dry.

Habit of Growth. A potato plant grows two to three feet tall and produces pretty purple flowers that resemble tomato blossoms in shape and form. Small potatoes form underground and you can enjoy your own minuscule crop.

Radish

Raphanus sativus
CRUCIFERAE

Origin. China. Radishes are mentioned very frequently in ancient writings. We know they were cultivated in Egypt at the time of the Pharaohs and we also know the Greeks made offerings of radishes to Apollo on gold plates, while turnips were offered on lead, and beets on silver.

In medieval Europe the radish was considered to have magical and medicinal properties. It was used to detect witches, cure madness and exorcise demons. More mundane uses were to cure headaches, shingles, eyeaches and pains in the joints and to remove warts and black-and-blue marks.

How to Grow. Buy only firm fresh radishes. Select an attractive bowl and add a one-inch layer of pebbles. Place a half-dozen small radishes root end down on the pebbles and add more pebbles to hold them in place. Add water up to the level of the pebbles and maintain the water at this level throughout the growth period. Keep the bowl in a bright light except when you want to use it elsewhere as decoration.

Habit of Growth. Green leaves grow from the top of the radish and a flower stalk may develop. The small crinkly green leaves contrast beautifully with the round red roots, and if the plants bloom, your dish garden is a sight to behold.

Radish dish gardens last only a few weeks, but because they are so easy to grow, you can always start a new one.

Summer Squash

Cucurbita pepo
CUCURBITACEAE

Origin. North and South America. When the first explorers came to the New World, they found the Indians growing different kinds of squash. The name comes from the Indian word *askutasquash*.

How to Grow. Remove the seeds from the squash and scrub off excess pulp. The seeds may be dried and stored for later use or planted immediately. Squash can suffer from transplant shock, so we recommend the use of Jiffy pellets (see p. 3). Take three moistened Jiffy pellets, remove enough of the moist peat to insert one squash seed per pellet, and cover with the peat you removed. Keep the pellets in a waterproof container so that you can moisten them regularly. Slip a plastic bag over the container.

When the seedlings show, remove the plastic bag and put the container in a sunny window. When roots protrude through the pellets it is time to transplant. For each pellet, fill a six-inch pot one third full with moist average soil mix, place a pellet on the soil and fill in around it, barely covering it with soil. Keep the pots in a sunny place, water regularly and fertilize every week.

Habit of Growth. The seeds germinate in less than a week. Outdoors, the plant develops strong spreading vines. Indoors the plant will be smaller, and heart-shaped leaves will trail down from the pot, with large yellow flowers appearing in three to six weeks.

There are two kinds of flowers: male and female. The former has only stamens containing pollen; the latter has a green bulge, which is the ovary, below the petals. Outdoors, bees transfer the pollen from the male flowers to the female, and soon after, the green ball begins to swell and change into a squash. Indoors, you will not have any fruit unless you do the fertilizing yourself. Take a small paintbrush and touch it to the pollen of a male flower, then touch the brush to the center of the female flower. Within a week, the fruit should begin to develop.

Sweet Potato

Ipomoea batatas
CONVOLVULACEAE

Origin. South and Central America. When Columbus came to America he found many varieties of sweet potato growing here. Today they are grown in tropical and subtropical countries throughout the world.

How to Grow. The difficult part is picking the right sweet potato. Many are dried in kilns or treated with special chemicals to keep them from sprouting. Go to a small vegetable store or a farmers' market and ask for help in choosing a sweet potato that has some sign of life, such as some roots or little purple buds.

Stick three toothpicks into the sides of the sweet potato about one third of the way down from the top (the top is rounder in shape than the bottom). Set the potato in a tall opaque jar of water with the toothpicks resting on the rim. Keep adding water to replenish what evaporates.

Set the jar on the windowsill in bright light in a *warm* place.

Habit of Growth. The roots come from the tapering bottom end of the potato, and most of the stem and leaf buds start at the top. The sweet potato is a vine and can cover a window in a short time with heart-shaped leaves, which resemble those of a morning glory except that the sweet potato leaves have lovely purple veins. The potato plant will last for months.

Turnip

Brassica rapa
CRUCIFERAE

Origin. Russia, Siberia and the Scandinavian peninsula. Turnips have been cultivated since ancient times. Greek writings describe some turnips as reaching a weight of a hundred pounds. The small white turnips we buy in our markets today were probably developed by the Dutch. The vegetable is now grown throughout the temperate and cooler regions of the world.

How to Grow. Select an attractive bowl and place a one-inch layer of pebbles in it. If the turnips are small, place two or three directly on the pebbles, root end down. If you are using one large turnip, cut off the bottom half and place the top half, cut side down, on the pebbles. Add more pebbles to hold the turnips in place. Add water to the level of the pebbles and maintain this water level throughout. Place the bowl in bright light.

Habit of Growth. Like carrots and beets, the turnip is a biennial. Planted indoors, it will produce a rosette of rough, curly green leaves that contrast nicely with the purple turnip tops. Small yellow flowers may appear which resemble the flowers of the mustard plant.

3
Plants from Common Fruits and Nuts

Any part of a plant that has a seed in it is technically a fruit. The avocado is a fruit, and so is a peanut or an almond.

The seeds inside a wide variety of fruits can produce interesting plants. Among these is the familiar avocado pit. But the seeds of even such fruits as apples, figs, dates and citrus fruit—lemons, oranges, and grapefruit—can grow into attractive botanical specimens. The pineapple grows into an exotic plant with long sword-shaped leaves. The date becomes a palm tree. The fig tree has interesting three-lobed leaves. Citrus seeds grow into beautiful small trees with shiny green leaves.

For something unusual, try growing a peanut. You can actually see the yellow flowers lose their petals, bend down and grow into the ground to form the peanuts.

Once you start growing these unusual plants you will think twice before throwing away a pineapple top or the seeds of any other fruit that might possibly grow.

Almond

Prunus amygdalus
ROSACEAE

Origin. North Africa and Asia. Almonds were enjoyed by both the ancient Hebrews and the seafaring Phoenicians. They are now grown in almost every country with a temperate climate.

How to Grow. The edible part of the almond is the pit of the almond fruit, which looks like a dried peach. When the fruit falls from the tree, the fibrous outer husk splits, and the nuts are removed from the husks.

Almonds do not germinate readily unless they are stratified (see p. 8). To accomplish this, put almonds either shelled or unshelled (both ways work) in a bag of moist peat moss. Place the bag in the refrigerator for six to eight weeks. Then plant one seed to each Jiffy pellet (see p. 3). With your fingers, remove enough peat so that you can place the almond horizontally and cover it with the peat you removed. Place the pellets in a dish so that it will be easy to moisten them regularly, and slip a plastic bag over the dish. When the seedlings show, remove the plastic bag and put the dish in a sunny window.

When roots fill the pellets, transplant each pellet to a four-inch pot: Fill one third of the pot with moist average soil mix, place the pellet on the soil and add enough soil to barely cover it.

Habit of Growth. After its spell in the refrigerator the almond grows with spectacular speed. It seems to jump by inches and becomes leggy very quickly. To keep the young tree shapely, cut back the main stem to encourage branching. The result will be a most unusual houseplant.

Apple

Malus sylvestris
ROSACEAE

Origin. Europe and Asia. Apples were introduced to America by the colonists from England. Many different varieties are found in most temperate regions of the world.

How to Grow. Apple seeds are difficult to germinate when taken fresh from the fruit, so we recommend stratification. Put the seeds in damp peat moss in a jar or plastic cup and cover it with plastic wrap. Leave the seeds in the refrigerator for about two months, checking once a week to make sure the peat moss is damp. After two months take them out and plant them in Jiffy pellets (see p. 3). When roots have filled the pellets, transfer each pellet to a four-inch pot: Fill the pot one third full with moist average soil, place the pellet on it and fill in around it, barely covering it.

Habit of Growth. Like most trees, apple trees grow slowly. In the winter, when their leaves drop, they should be kept in a cold place, such as an outside windowsill. Remember to water about once very two weeks. Your tree will never bear fruit, but it will be long-lived and lovely to look at.

Peaches, pears, plums and nectarines should be treated the same way as apples: they require stratification and a cool winter.

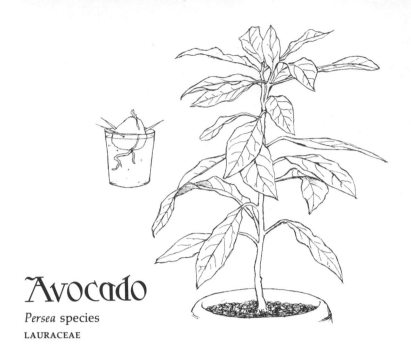

Avocado

Persea species
LAURACEAE

Origin. Central and South America and the West Indies.

How to Grow. There are two main types of avocados. The larger, grown in Florida, has shiny dark-green skins and a pit which germinates quite readily—in fact, you often find it with roots already started. Avocados from California are smaller and rounder and can be green and smooth or nubby and purple. The pit is smaller and more difficult to germinate. Within these two groups there are over four hundred hybrids. Use only ripe or, even better, overripe fruit. Scrub the pit to remove the brown skin and any residue of flesh. Pierce the middle of the pit with three toothpicks and place it in a glass of water with the flat end down so that the bottom third of the pit is covered by water. Change the water weekly and maintain the water level. Put the glass in a warm place out of strong light.

Germination time varies with each pit, but the average time is a few weeks. If the roots are already started when you open the avocado, germination takes very little time. But sometimes a pit will linger for months and sprout only as you are about to throw it out.

An interesting variation on the usual way of starting avocado pits is to put them in a plastic bag containing moist peat. Fold up the bag and put it in a warm place. In a few weeks you will probably find the bag full of roots and shoots.

When the roots are three to four inches long, transfer the avocado to a pot one inch larger than the pit. Fill the pot one third full with a moist average soil mix. Gently place the pit on the soil and fill in enough soil around it so that half the pit is exposed at the top. Place the pot in a warm bright spot (avocados do not require direct sunlight).

Keep the soil moist, but not soggy, at all times. During their natural resting period from October to January, avocados need less water. As soon as the days lengthen, new leaves will appear; then you can start to water more.

Habit of growth. Once established, avocados grow quite rampantly. Most of them develop a small cluster of leaves around a six-inch stem, which grows taller and taller without producing any branches. In order to encourage branching, the usual technique is to cut the stem back to within three inches of the pit. However, in our experience each time the stem is cut back it sprouts a branch which takes over the lead, leaving you with not only another unbranching stem but also a stump where the original stem was cut off. If you do this enough times, your plant will begin to look like a hat rack. Our suggestion is to let the avocado go its own way until, about a year later, it starts to branch naturally. At this time you can trim the side branches to make the plant more shapely.

When grown properly, the avocado can become one of the most beautiful plants in your home. We have a thirty-six-inch barrel into which we have set ten avocados in varying stages of development. It forms a cool refreshing grove at the end of the living room.

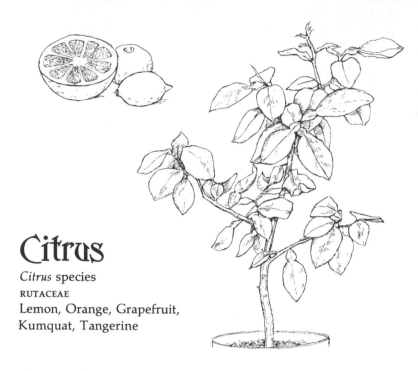

Citrus

Citrus species
RUTACEAE
Lemon, Orange, Grapefruit,
Kumquat, Tangerine

Origin. India, China, Indochina and Burma.

How to Grow. Select ripe fruit and plant the seeds immediately in Jiffy pellets (p. 3)—one seed to each pellet. With your fingers, remove enough peat to place each seed in the soil and cover it with the peat you remove. Keep the pellets in a dish to which you can add water so that you can moisten them regularly. Slip a plastic bag over the dish.

The seeds should sprout in two to three weeks. When the seedlings show, remove the plastic bag and put the dish in a sunny window.

As soon as roots fill the pellets transplant them to four-inch pots filled one third full with a moist average soil mix to which a pinch of lime or broken eggshell has been added. Place a pellet in each pot and barely cover it with soil. Place the pots in the sunniest spot you have available.

Habit of Growth. Outdoors citrus trees may grow as high as twenty-five feet. Indoors the plant can become ten feet high. Actually, the height depends on the size of the pot and the amount of fertilizing you do. Citrus trees are slow growers—about a foot a year. They branch naturally, and, with their dark glossy leaves, make beautiful houseplants. With enough time and sun, flowers may appear.

Date

Phoenix dactylifera
PALMACEAE

Origin. North Africa and Arabia. The date palm has been cultivated for over four thousand years. John the Baptist described four varieties in his trek through the wilderness. Today it is still an important staple in Middle Eastern diets.

How to Grow. For several years we had difficulty germinating the packaged supermarket dates, but now we have discovered dates that will grow easily. These are the light golden-brown dates that have been cured in the sun and not in kilns. They are never packaged and are advertised in many ways—"unpasteurized," "non-sulfured," "natural" and "imported." They are not as sticky as those commonly bought in packages.

A very simple method using Jiffy pellets has yielded us 100 percent germination. Insert the seeds, one to a pellet, making sure they are entirely covered with peat. Cover the pellets with a plastic bag and give them a high bottom heat of 80 degrees (see p. 8). Frequently the first sign of growth is a large taproot protruding from the bottom of the pellet. Within three to six weeks a small linear leaf will appear, and it is time to transplant. Using four-inch pots filled with two inches of a moist average soil mix, place a pellet in each pot, fill in around it with more soil and barely cover it.

Habit of Growth. Palms are very slow growers, and the

date palm is no exception. After sitting around looking at one linear leaf for a year, only to be rewarded with two linear leaves the next, we became discouraged. At the price of New York real estate, these were turning into very expensive and not very attractive plants. Luckily, we were given a hint from a kitchen gardener in Washington, D.C., who has an absolutely magnificent six-year-old date palm. She said she starts all her dates in the soil at the base of other large plants and just lets them stay there until they are attractive enough to warrant a pot of their own.

Palms are ideally suited for the low humidity found in most American homes and require relatively little attention. Contrary to what you might imagine, they do not need full sunlight and are even likely to scorch with too much sun. They must be watered whenever the top soil seems dry, because they do require considerable water. Palms have been known to grow for over a hundred years, and while progress may be slow at first, this is a plant you can pass on to your grandchildren.

Fig

Ficus carica

MORACEAE

Origin. Near East and North Africa.

How to Grow. Buy Smyrna figs, available in health food stores. (The seeds of this type of fig are fertile and can grow into new plants, while the seeds of the common fig have no embryos and cannot grow.) Remove from a fig the pulp containing the seeds and put it in a small bowl of water. With your fingers, separate as much pulp as possible from the seed, then pour off the water and add more clean water. By the next morning most of the remaining pulp will have dissolved, and the tiny seeds will be at the bottom of the bowl. Pour off the water carefully to retain the seeds.

To plant these seeds, fill a plastic dish half full with soilless mix, and using a spoon, pick up a few seeds at a time and press them into the mix. Slip a plastic bag over the dish and set it in a warm place.

When the seedlings are four inches high, select the best ones to grow into large-size plants. To remove a seedling from the dish, gently loosen the soil underneath it with a pencil and lift it out by the leaves. For each seedling, fill a four-inch pot with an average soil mix (see p. 5) and, using the pencil, make a hole deep enough to receive the roots. Cover about an inch of the stem with soil. Water well and place the pot in a sunny window.

To advance to larger pots, follow instructions on p. 9.

Habit of Growth: Fig trees grow fairly rapidly. Their large, deeply lobed leaves look exotic and contrast with the somewhat brown angular stem. They make rather large indoor plants and can be transferred to the garden provided they are protected in the winter.

Peanut

Arachis hypogaae
LEGUMINOSAE

Origin. South America. The peanut plant has traveled all over the world from its first home in South America. Because many varieties seemed to be native to Asia and Africa, the peanut's origin was unclear until tombs more than fifteen hundred years old in Peru were found to contain jars with peanut designs on them.

How to Grow. First be sure to get fresh *unroasted* peanuts—the kind you buy in a seed store or in some old-fashioned vegetable stores. Remove the shells and plant four peanuts in a moist average soil mix (see p. 5) in a six-inch pot. Cover the peanuts with about an inch of soil. After the plants have germinated and grown to a height of four inches, remove all but the sturdiest plant.

Habit of Growth. The peanut is a pretty plant with oval leaves, and grows to a height of one or two feet. At night the leaves fold up into a "sleeping" position, which children will find especially interesting. The yellow flowers look like small sweet peas. After the flower is pollinated (it pollinates itself), the petals fall off, the ovary swells and starts to grow down toward the ground, and then it pushes into the earth and changes into a peanut containing two seeds. A clear plastic pot will permit you to watch this unusual process if the seeds are planted close to the outer edge of the pot.

Pineapple

Ananas comosus
BROMELIACEAE

Origin. Tropical America. In 1493 Columbus saw pine-apples in the West Indies, where they had been brought from South America. Within fifty years pineapples were intro-duced all over the world by the Spanish and the Portuguese.

How to Grow. There are two commercial varieties of pineapple on the market. The smooth, or Hawaiian, pineap-ple is available year round and accounts for 75 percent of the crops raised. Its leaves are spineless. The other kind, the vigorous Queen Abakka pineapple, is available only in late summer and early fall. It has narrower spiny leaves. At the base of the crown it will have a cluster of basal shoots which can be broken off and rooted in sand, giving as many as ten plants for the price of one.

To begin with, look for a pineapple, either Hawaiian or Abakka, with fresh center leaves in the crown. If you have to keep a pineapple for a few days before eating it, sprinkle the crown with water to keep the leaves fresh. Cut off the crown of leaves where it meets the fruit, *leaving no fruit on it.* Then peel off the bottom half-dozen leaves. Place the crown in a narrow jar filled with enough water to cover the bottom of the crown.

In two to three weeks, when roots appear, the pineapple

can be transferred to a pot. Cover at least one inch of the bottom of the crown with a moist average soil mix.

Habit of Growth. If you imagine the crown of a pineapple as being six times bigger than it is, you will have an idea of what a pineapple looks like growing in the field. Indoors a pineapple plant will grow to at least half that size.

We believe the Queen Abakka variety grows into a more exotic-looking plant than the Hawaiian type, but both make striking foliage plants.

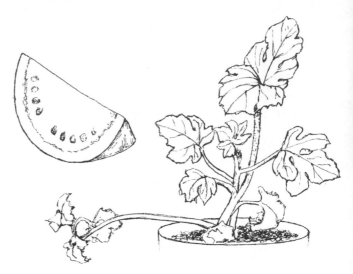

Watermelon

Citrullus vulgaris
CUCURBITACEAE

Origin. Africa. In Africa today you can still find whole areas covered with wild watermelon plants. The fruit has adapted well to cultivation in America, and now there are many varieties.

How to Grow. Rinse the seeds from a ripe watermelon and plant one or two per moistened Jiffy pellet. Remove enough peat so that you can plant the seeds and cover them with the peat you removed. Set the pellets in a dish to which you can add water to keep them constantly moist. Cover the dish with a plastic bag and set in a warm place. When the seedlings show, move the dish to a sunny location. In a week or two the seedlings will be a few inches tall, and you can transfer each pellet into a four-inch pot with an average soil mix. From then on, water daily and feed each week with liquid fertilizer.

You can also make a hanging basket of watermelon vines. Fill a plastic hanging pot with an average soil mix to within an inch of the top. Then place about ten seeds on the soil mix about one inch apart and cover them with a quarter of an inch of the mix. Water the pot so that the mix is just moist. Cover with a large plastic bag and set the pot in a sunny place. When the seeds germinate, remove the plastic bag. Water daily and fertilize every week with liquid fertilizer.

Habit of Growth. Outdoors watermelon is a large strong vine that scrambles over the ground. Indoors it is a much smaller plant, but it looks interesting because of its deeply lobed leaves. If the plant is kept in full sun, there will be large yellow flowers.

4

Plants from Herbs and Spices

Charlemagne described herbs as "the friend of physicians and the pride of the cook." And, we would humbly add, the joy of the kitchen gardener. Many are beautiful to look at and most offer a harvestable crop.

For thousands of years herbs were the only medicines available to man. Today herbs are still used in the treatment of various illnesses, as, for instance, foxglove (the source of digitalis) in the management of heart disease.

As to cooking with herbs, there are hundreds of books that tell you to use rosemary with chicken, dill with fish, etc. Our thoughts on the subject are best expressed by Irma Rombauer, the author of *The Joy of Cooking:* "My rules are elastic ... Epicures are insistent upon the wedding of the right herb to the right dish and in some circles, only the brave venture forth on a doubtful alliance. However, a break in the conventions cannot be much worse than a split infinitive or a double negative and they certainly have been known to creep into the best of families." We agree, and advise that you let your nose and common sense be your guide. When herbs and spices are used with discretion, marvelous new flavors can be added to old standard dishes.

Horticulturally, herbs have become all the rage. Many bazaars, flower shows and church fairs offer plantings of herbs for the windowsill, sometimes with seven or eight varieties crowded into a single container. But while these lovely collections, offered at astronomical prices, may have done beautifully in the grower's greenhouse or garden, their performance in your home is another matter altogether. And then there are the elegant Christmas catalogs offering kits for the indoor gardener, again at horrendous prices. Stay away from all this nonsense. Herbs are available everywhere. They are cheap. And most of all, they are easy to grow.

The next time you are at your grocery store, look carefully at the herb and spice shelves and you will notice that many of them are seeds. Most will grow, some will bloom and a few will actually yield seeds. Anise, caraway, celery, coriander, dill, fennel, mustard and sesame are easily found. You do not have to send away for them or let anybody else do your growing for you.

Many of these plants are members of Umbelliferae, a family of plants which is probably best known for its Queen Anne's lace, the plant with flat-topped clusters of beautiful lacy flowers that later turn to seed. Outdoors insects do the job of transferring pollen from one flower to another, but indoors, you will have to do it yourself in order to have seeds. The pollen is ready to be transferred if it comes off on your hand when you touch the flowers. Simply take a small sheet of paper and shake the flowers over it; then hold the paper above the same flowers and shake the pollen onto them.

Some herbs are rapid growers—the tender young leaves of the mustard plant can be harvested in four days. Others take more time, but all are worth a try. Most important, it's fun and easy to grow these plants. It's also great fun to use herbs as decorative centerpieces for the dining table and to let your guests snip and taste the pungent foliage.

Anise

Pimpinella anisum
UMBELLIFERAE

Origin. Greece, Crete and Egypt. Anise was listed as a medicinal plant in the Ebers Papyrus, a famous Egyptian medical manuscript dating back to 1500 B.C. The Greeks considered anise a medicine, and the Romans favored its use in many seasonings and sauces. The old herbals say that anise is both a stimulant and a relaxant, and that it is also an aromatic, diaphoretic and tonic, besides being helpful for lung and stomach troubles. Today it is still used as a home remedy. A few drops of oil supposedly help stomach ailments, and the oil added to hot water is used to help relieve asthma and bronchitis. Anethole, the oil of anise, is used in modern cough mixtures.

How to Grow. Plant four anise seeds in a moistened Jiffy pellet: Remove a little of the peat and cover the seeds with the peat you removed. Put the pellet in a dish that can hold water so that you can moisten the pellet regularly, and slip a plastic bag over the container. When the seedlings show, which should be within a week or two, remove the plastic bag and put the pellet in a cool sunny window.

After roots fill the pellet, transfer it to a four-inch flower pot filled a third full with a moist average soil mix (see p. 5). Place the pellet on the soil, fill in around it and barely cover it with soil. Keep the pot in bright sun. The seedlings do not transplant well, so when they are a few inches tall, thin them out, allowing only one plant per pot.

Habit of Growth. Anise seeds germinate in one week. The first leaves are round and toothed, but later leaves are deeply lobed. The flowers, which appear later, are white, delicate and lacy like those of Queen Anne's lace. To produce seeds, pollinate as described on p. 37.

Outdoors anise grows to a height of two feet. Indoors it seldom becomes more than a foot tall.

As Food. The seeds, which have a distinctive licorice flavor, are used in bread, pastries, candies and liqueurs, such as anisette, Pernod, and ouzo. In India it is used in some curries, and is also chewed after meals to sweeten the breath and supposedly to cure indigestion.

The leaves are used in salads and stews, and the French like them especially with carrots.

Caraway

Carum carvi
UMBELLIFERAE

Origin. Asia Minor. Caraway is named after the ancient state of Caria, which is now part of Turkey, where it probably grew wild.

Caraway is one of the oldest cultivated herbs in the world. Seeds have been found around the homes of Swiss lake dwellers dating back to 5000 B.C. For centuries caraway was used to cure just about every human ailment from "women's-falling-down sickness to breaking wind."

How to Grow. Remove a little of the peat of a moistened Jiffy pellet and plant four seeds, covering them with the peat you removed. Keep the pellet in a dish that holds water so that you can moisten the pellet regularly. Slip a plastic bag over the container.

When the seedlings show, which should be within a week, remove the plastic bag and put the container in a sunny window.

When roots fill the pellet, transfer it to a four-inch flower pot. Fill it one third full with a moist average soil mix (see p. 5). Place the pellet on the soil, fill in around it and barely cover it with soil. Place the pot in a bright sunny window. The seedlings do not transplant well, so when they are a few inches tall, thin them out, allowing only one plant per pot.

Habit of Growth. Outside caraway attains a height of two feet. Potbound in the home, it will be a smaller, more compact plant. It has dissected, feathery foliage like that of the carrot plant, and its bloom resembles that of Queen Anne's lace. To produce your own caraway seeds, pollinate as described on p. 37.

As Food. Caraway seed is used to flavor liqueurs and cordials, the most famous being the German kümmel. The seeds are also used sprinkled on rye bread and cookies and as flavoring for pastries and cheeses. A favorite recipe of ours is cabbage wedges cooked until just tender and tossed gently with butter and caraway seeds.

The foliage of the young plants adds a pungent and unusual flavor to soups and salads and can also be chopped and sprinkled fresh on vegetables and meats.

Celery

Apium graveolens
UMBELLIFERAE

Origin. Europe and Asia. As a wild plant it grows in marshy places. As a result of centuries of cultivation, celery has become transformed from a bitter plant to the sweet crisp vegetable we know. Much of the credit for this goes to the Italians.

How to Grow. Take a moistened Jiffy pellet, remove a little of the peat and plant four celery seeds, covering them with the peat you removed. Put the pellet in a dish to which you can add water to keep the pellets constantly moist, and slip a plastic bag over the dish.

When the seedlings show, which should be within a week, remove the plastic bag and put the dish in a sunny window.

When roots fill the pellet, transfer the pellet to a four-inch flower pot. Fill it a third full with a moist average soil mix (see p. 5). Place the pellet on the soil, fill in around it and barely cover it with soil. Place the pot in a bright sunny window. The seedlings do not transplant well, so when they are a few inches tall, thin them out, leaving only one plant per pot.

Habit of Growth. Imagine the familiar celery leaves at the top of the stalks spread out and green, and you will have a good idea of what the celery plant looks like. Indoors the plant will not produce the thick stalks you buy in the store because these require special cultivation. The plant is a biennial and will not produce flowers the first year. If you keep the plant long enough you should get small white flowers that resemble Queen Anne's lace. Pollinate, as described on p. 37, to produce your own seeds.

As Food. The stalks are a common vegetable, and the seeds can be used for flavoring soups and salads.

Coriander

Coriandrum sativum
UMBELLIFERAE

Origin. Europe and Asia. Coriander seeds have been found in Egyptian tombs, and the Chinese were also using them three thousand years ago. In ancient Rome they were used to preserve meat.

How to Grow. Remove a little of the peat from a moistened Jiffy pellet, plant four seeds and cover them with the peat you removed. Put the pellet in a dish that can hold water so that you can moisten the pellet regularly. Slip a plastic bag over the container. When the seedlings show, which should be within a week, remove the plastic bag and put the dish in a sunny window.

When roots fill the pellet, transfer to a four-inch pot. Fill it one third full with a moist average soil mix (see p. 5). Place the pellet on the soil, fill in around it and barely cover it with soil. Place the pot in a bright sunny window. The seedlings do not transplant well, so when they are a few inches high, thin them out, leaving only one.

Habit of Growth. The lobed lower leaves of this plant contrast nicely with the feathery upper ones. Grown in a sunny window, the coriander will produce clusters of lovely lavender or pink flowers. If you would like to produce your own seeds indoors, try the pollination method described on p. 37.

As Food. Coriander seeds are a basic ingredient of curry and chutney. Also known as Chinese parsley, the leaves are popular in Chinese dishes. Used as a spice and a seasoning since antiquity.

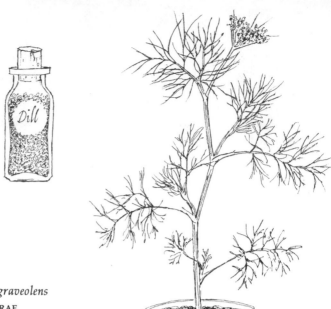

Dill

Anethum graveolens
UMBELLIFERAE

Origin. Europe and Asia. Used since ancient times, dill was once thought to keep people thin and to cure hiccoughs. Interestingly, although it was used in some places as a remedy for insomnia, in colonial times people took dill seed to church to nibble on to keep them awake.

How to Grow. To plant the seeds directly into a moistened Jiffy pellet (see p. 3), remove about an inch or so of peat, place four seeds about an inch apart, cover them with the peat. Keep the pellet in a dish that can hold water so that you can moisten the pellet regularly. Slip a plastic bag over the pellet and dish and tie the bag.

When the seedlings show, which should be within a week, remove the plastic bag and put the container in a cool sunny window.

When the roots fill the pellet, transfer it to a four-inch flower pot. Fill the pot one third full with a moist average soil mix (see p. 5). Place the pellet on the soil, fill in around it and barely cover it with soil. Place the pot in a sunny window. The seedlings do not transplant well, so when they are a few inches tall, thin them out, leaving only one plant in the pot.

Habit of Growth. Within four weeks you should have lovely feathery foliage which can be snipped into salads and soups. Two to three weeks later, clusters of greenish-yellow flowers resembling Queen Anne's lace will develop if the plant has had adequate sunlight. To produce seed, pollinate as described on p. 37. A healthy plant will be about twelve to eighteen inches high.

Fennel

Foeniculum vulgare
UMBELLIFERAE

Origin. European shores of the Mediterranean. Fennel has been cultivated for over three thousand years. In ancient Greece and Rome sprigs of fennel were used to crown victorious warriors.

How to Grow. Like many other members of the Umbelliferae family, fennel is difficult to transplant. Therefore, we strongly recommend starting them in Jiffy pellets (see p. 3). Remove a little peat from a moistened pellet, plant four seeds and cover with the peat you removed. Keep the pellet in a dish that can hold water so that you can moisten the pellet regularly. Slip a plastic bag over the dish. When the seedlings show, remove the plastic bag and place the dish in a sunny window.

When the seedlings are a few inches tall, thin them out, leaving only one plant per pot. When the roots fill the pellet, transfer the pellet to a four-inch flower pot. Fill it one third full with a moist average soil mix (see p. 5). Place the pellet on the soil, fill in around it and barely cover it with soil.

Habit of Growth. Fennel is a graceful but rangy plant. The leaves are finely divided into threadlike pale-green segments. The stalks are a green-blue and the flowers, which appear in about six weeks, are a pale yellow-green.

Fennel needs full sun and lots of water. It is relatively

hardy and can be grown on a cool windowsill. If you wish to harvest seeds, follow the instructions for pollination on p. 37. One umbel, or cluster of flowers, alone can yield twenty to thirty seeds.

As food. The leaves have a delicate licorice flavor and are used in salads, sauces, soups and meat dishes.

The seeds contain a volatile oil which is used to flavor bread, pastry, candy, liqueurs and meat.

Fenugreek

Trigonella foenum-graecum
LEGUMINOSAE

Origin. Southern Europe and Asia. The word literally translates into "Greek hay." Although the plant bears no resemblance to hay, it is used for fodder in much of the Mediterranean world.

How to Grow. Fill a six-inch pot three quarters full with a moist average soil mix (see p. 5). Place six seeds on the soil and cover them with a quarter inch of soil. Slip a plastic bag over the pot and set it in a warm place. When the seeds germinate (in three to ten days), remove the plastic bag and place the pot in a sunny window. Water as needed to keep the soil moist.

Habit of Growth. Fenugreek is a small, attractive trailing plant with leaves that resemble those of the pea family. Small white pea-like flowers appear within eight weeks. They self-pollinate and are followed shortly by bean-like pods.

Fenugreek makes a pretty hanging basket when several seeds are grown in the pot as described.

As Food. The seeds make an exotic spice that is found in almost all Middle and Far Eastern markets. They were a gastronomic discovery for us. We have used them in chicken stock, scattered them in the bottom of roasting pans with pork or chicken to enrich the gravy and, best of all, inserted the seeds in lamb before roasting.

Fenugreek is a component of curry in India. In Turkey and Iraq it is used with paprika to preserve meat.

BLACK
MUSTARD
SEED

Mustard

Brassica species
CRUCIFERAE

Origin. Europe and Asia. Since antiquity mustard seeds have been used to cure ailments as well as to preserve perishables. Today mustard poultices are used as a household remedy for bronchitis and muscular aches and pains.

How to Grow. Fill a shallow plastic container three-fourths full with a moist soilless mix (see p. 5). Scatter a tablespoonful of seeds evenly on the surface. Cover the seeds with a light dusting of soil and then slip a plastic bag over the container. Put the container in a warm, sunny window. The seeds germinate rapidly. Remove the bag when the seedlings are four inches high.

If you want to grow a plant to maturity, remove one seedling from the plastic container by gently loosening the soil underneath the seedling with a pencil and lifting the plant out by the leaves. (A plant can always regenerate new leaves but not a stem.) Fill a four-inch pot with an average soil mix. Use the pencil to make a hole deep enough to receive the roots, and cover about an inch of the stem with soil. Water well and place the pot in a sunny window.

Habit of Growth. When not crowded, the mustard plant will grow to a height of two feet. The foliage is rough but attractive and the plant will produce four-petaled yellow flowers if the light is good.

As Food. Mustard has many uses. Cut when the plant is three inches high, the young leaves are a tasty garnish for steaks, salads and soups. The rougher older leaves are cooked like spinach, but mustard greens are much tangier in taste. The seed is ground to make the mustard powder used in the condiment for the table, and the whole seed is used as pickling spice.

Sesame

Sesamum indicum

PEDALINEAE

Origin. Asia and Africa. The famous phrase "Open Sesame" probably comes from the fact that the seed capsules split open when ripe. Because the leaves are mucilaginous and sticky, they were used as a remedy for cholera, dysentery and diarrhea.

How to Grow. Fill a shallow plastic container three-fourths full with a moist soilless mix (see p. 5). Scatter a tablespoonful of seeds evenly on the surface. Cover the seeds with a light dusting of the mix and then slip a plastic bag over the container. Put the container in a sunny window.

The seeds germinate rapidly and will be several inches high in two weeks. Sesame plants are most attractive when crowded together in their original container, and they can stay this way for months.

If you want to grow a plant to maturity, you must transplant one seedling. To do this, gently loosen the soil underneath a seedling with a pencil and lift the plant out by the leaves. Fill a four-inch pot with an average soil mix (see p. 5). Use the pencil to make a hole deep enough to receive the roots, and cover about an inch of the stem with soil. Water well and place in a sunny window.

Habit of Growth. Though attractive, the sesame plant is a somewhat weedy-looking annual. The leaves are oval and slightly hairy. In a sunny window you will have tubular pinkish-white flowers, which resemble foxglove. The flowers are self-pollinating and will be followed by seed capsules that will pop open when ripe.

As Food. The seeds with their nutty taste may be scattered over bread and cakes or used in candies and desserts. Halvah, a famous sweet of the Middle East, is made of ground sesame. Tahina, a paste made from the seeds, is used in salad dressing or to flavor cooked chickpeas in a dish called hummus. The oil expressed from the seeds is an excellent salad oil, and is much used in Japan.

5
Plants from Latin American Markets

We set forth from our Manhattan apartments on our first field trip in pursuit of Latin American tubers. Within two blocks we struck gold: in a small Puerto Rican grocery store we found glorious boxes full of all the tubers we were looking for and more.

The big problem with tubers is which end is up and which down. Milly, the botanist, peeled back the skin of each strange object in search of the growing end and to evaluate the viability of each tuber. The proprietors found her behavior somewhat alarming and soon we had a curious audience. Milly's Spanish vocabulary was limited to "What is it?" and "How do you spell it?" Neither went very far to explain her actions, but she did manage to convince them that we were harmless, albeit a little crazy. Soon we were all chatting in English and Spanish.

Out of all the confusion one fact emerged: some tubers have several different names. The vegetable Debbie called malanga, Milly called a dasheen and the proprietor called a yautia. The owners assured us that all the names were correct, that some were Puerto Rican, others Mexican, and some Spanish. We think we have straightened all this out and whenever possible we will give other ethnic names. Our taxonomy is based on L. H. Bailey's *Cyclopedia of Horticulture.*

We each purchased two of each item, one to eat and one to grow, since we grow things slightly differently and wanted to find which was the better technique. By the way, these ethnic markets are not cheap. Ñames, which in the tropics are a substitute for potatoes, cost as much as fifty-nine cents a pound.

Chayote

Sechium edule
CUCURBITACEAE

Origin. Mexico and Guatemala. Chayote was cultivated by Central American Indians long before the discovery of America.

Description. The fruit is green or cream-colored and resembles a deeply ribbed squash. The seed usually protrudes at the upper end of the fruit. Frequently the seeds are already sprouting when you buy the fruit. It is available year round in Latin American groceries.

How to Grow. Plant the entire fruit horizontally in a pot big enough to contain it. Use an average soil mix (see p. 5) and cover the fruit with the soil. Slip a plastic bag over the pot and put in a warm place. When you see growth starting, remove the plastic bag and put the pot in a bright or sunny window. Keep the plant well watered and fertilize it often with plant food.

Habit of Growth. The chayote is a vigorous vine. Outdoors it can grow fifty feet in one season. While it will not bloom indoors, it can easily cover a window with its cucumber-like lobed leaves.

As Food. Chayote can be cooked like summer squash.

Malanga

Xanthosoma sagittifolium
ARACEAE

Origin. South and Central America.

Description. The name malanga is used interchangeably with the names yautia and dasheen. It should not be confused with the dasheen sold in Chinese markets (see Chinese dasheen, p. 105). They are two different horticultural species requiring different growing conditions.

The Latin American malanga is a pinkish-brown tuber ranging in size from four to ten inches long and two to three inches wide. It is banded by narrow horizontal gray stripes and usually tapers to a tip at one end. It is available year round in Latin American grocery stores.

How to Grow. We recommend starting the tuber in a peat moss bag (see p. 6). When using this technique, you should check every three or four days for any soft spots that might develop and cut them out at once.

In one to three weeks pointed pink buds will sprout all over the tuber. When the buds are one to two inches long, it is time to plant the tuber. (You need not wait for roots to appear.)

Fill a shallow pot (wide enough to accommodate the tuber with an inch to spare all around) half full with a moist average soil mix (see p. 5). Place the tuber horizontally on the surface, and fill in around it and barely cover the tuber with more moist soil. Don't worry about the sprouts you have buried—they will work their way to the surface.

In the early stages of growth, the malanga needs high humidity and warmth. Once you have planted the tuber, cover the potted plant with a plastic bag and put it in a warm spot. When a few of the buds turn into leaves you may remove the plastic bag and place the plant in a bright window.

Habit of Growth. In nature malangas grow in jungles or open fields. They need plenty of moisture and warmth, but the amount of light they require can vary. Indoors the malanga develops into a compact leafy plant, seldom exceeding twelve inches in height. The leaves are a soft green and range in size from two to six inches long. Each leaf develops from the main stalk; as one leaf matures another peels off from the same stalk.

The malanga will do well in a shady part of the garden in summer or in a tub on the terrace as long as there is plenty of warmth and moisture. It can produce new small tubers underground.

As Food. The malanga is cooked much the same way as a sweet potato, boiled, peeled and mashed. It has a pleasant nutty flavor, but sometimes it can have a very slight sulfuric taste, which can be removed by adding lots of butter, salt, pepper and a dash of orange juice.

Mango
Mangifera indica
ANACARDIACEAE

Origin. India and Southeast Asia; now cultivated throughout all the tropical regions of the world.

The mango has been described as the "king of fruits," the "apple of the tropics," as well as "a ball of tow, soaked in turpentine and molasses and you have to eat it in the bathtub." As these quotes indicate, there are many varieties of diverse quality.

Description. Mangoes vary greatly in size and color; some are bright yellow and no larger than a peach, while others are bright green tinged with red and can weigh as much as four pounds. The commonest are oval in shape with waxy, thick skins. When properly ripe, the flesh, which is orange and creamy, will yield to the touch, and the fruit will give off a sweet perfume. Poor-quality mangoes have a slight odor of turpentine and are very fibrous, but even these make good plants. In the summer and fall they are found in good urban and suburban supermarkets, and occasionally appear in ethnic markets in the off season.

How to Grow. Within the mango there is a large hairy husk, which must be scrubbed so that it can be easily handled. At best, this is a very messy business. Scraping with a serrated steak knife speeds up the process, but you will still need a lot of paper towels and running water. Having cleaned the husk, let it dry out overnight.

The next day, clip off a tiny piece of the husk where there is a slight indentation. Then insert the point of a small knife and work it back and forth until you can grasp the edges of the husk and pry it apart. Care should be taken at all times to avoid hurting the seed (which looks like a large cashew nut) inside the husk.

Mango seeds may be germinated in several ways. The most usual way is to plant the seed horizontally in a pot some two inches wider than the seed. Use a moist average soil mix (see p. 5). Bury the seed a quarter inch beneath the surface of the soil. Tent the pot with plastic and put it in a warm place. A bottom heat (see p. 8) of 80 degrees will greatly speed germination. In ten days to three weeks you can look forward to seeing your first sprout.

We have had equal success sprouting the seeds in a peat moss bag (see p. 6). Seeds treated this way develop enormous roots in two to three weeks. Using a six-inch pot half filled with a moist average soil mix, place the sprouted seed on the soil. (You will have no trouble deciding which end is down because the roots and shoots will have formed by the time you plant it.) Fill in around the seed and cover it with a quarter inch of soil.

In the early stages of growth, the seedlings should be sheltered from direct sun. We stuck ours in among larger plants or grew them under light units.

Habit of Growth. The first leaves, which develop slowly, are not the usual dull basal leaves of the average plant. The plant sends up a palmate cluster of scarlet leaves atop a straight red stem. It is truly beautiful from the first day of its life. The leaves slowly change from red to chartreuse to a deep glossy green, and as they change color they also grow in size. There will be two to three growth spurts during the first year of a mango's life. Each time it will put out a cluster of five red leaves. (*Do not pinch off any leaves*—you will simply stall its growth.)

By the third year your mango will put out branches. Where it used to send out a cluster of five leaves, it will now develop five branches. Growth periods will be limited to once a year. When the lower leaves along the main trunk yellow and fall off, do not be distressed—this is a natural pattern.

In three years you will have a lovely (though non-fruit-bearing) tropical evergreen tree about four to five feet in height with umbrella-like branches and glossy green fluted leaves eight to twelve inches long.

The mango is one of the most challenging of "kitchen plants" and one of the most rewarding.

As Food. Mangoes are delicious eaten by themselves, mixed in fruit compotes or used in relishes such as chutney.

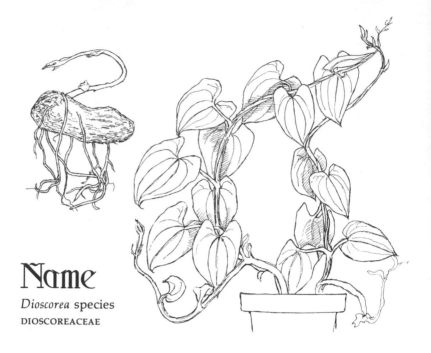

Ñame

Dioscorea species
DIOSCOREACEAE

Origin. Widely dispersed throughout the tropical regions of the world.

Description. Ñames come in the most incredible shapes and sizes. We have one in our collection which is the shape of an oversized foot, and another in the shape of a baseball mitt. Ñames are the biggest of all the tubers, some weighing as much as six pounds. They are found year round in Latin American grocery stores.

How to Grow. Our most successful method has been to put the ñame in a bag containing moist peat moss (see p. 6) and to place the bag over heat in a warm dark place. Care should be taken to look for soft spots, which should be removed at once because they can cause rot. Do not transfer to a pot until the vining stems are two to four inches long and a healthy root system has developed.

Select a pot six to eight inches across and deep enough to contain the tuber vertically. Put one to two inches of a moist average soil mix (see p. 5) in the pot, place the tuber vertically on the soil (stems up, roots down) and fill in around the tuber with more moist soil, barely covering the top of the tuber. Place in a warm bright window.

Habit of Growth. Ñames are very vigorous vines, and once established they can grow at the extraordinary rate of a foot a day. Give them plenty of room and supports on which to trail. A ñame casually left at home for a weekend can strangle a nearby avocado or wrap itself around a television set. Their vigor cannot be overstressed.

Ideally, ñames should be grown in full sun for the best leaf color, but they do well in any bright location. They need daily waterings because of their enormous size. Small new tubers will form underground.

Ñame shapes are so large and interesting that we have used the tubers as table decorations. Some we had kept around the house for several months suddenly started sprouting buds without the aid of soil, heat or light. This phenomenon started in May and is probably related to the normal growth cycle of the plant. When this happened we reluctantly parted with our *objets d'art* and put them in the peat bag to encourage root growth.

As Food. Ñames are a bit fibrous and tough for American tastes, but their flavor is similar to that of the sweet potato, and they can be cooked the same way—boiled, peeled and mashed (we suggest using a blender because of their fibrousness).

Papaya

Carica papaya
CARICACEAE

Origin. Central America. Indians have long used papayas to cure indigestion and to tenderize their meat. The active substance is papain, an enzyme, which today is the most important ingredient in commercial meat tenderizers.

Description. A large pear-shaped fruit eight to ten inches long, the papaya is usually sold green, but it turns yellow when ripe. To ripen, keep in a warm dark part of the kitchen. The papaya is found year round in Latin American markets and during the spring, summer and fall in better supermarkets.

How to Grow. When you slice the papaya, you will see enough seeds to start a plantation. The dark-brown seeds are surrounded by a gelatinous sac called the aril. To remove the aril, roll the seeds with your fingers on a paper towel until the crinkled brown seed pops out.

Use moistened Jiffy pellets (see p. 3) to plant the seeds. Remove enough peat to plant two or three seeds in the pellets, and cover them with the peat you removed. Put the pellets into a shallow container that can hold water so that you can moisten the pellets regularly. Slip the container into a plastic bag, and place it over bottom heat (see p. 8).

When the seeds germinate (this will happen within two weeks), remove the plastic bag and put the container where it is bright but not sunny. Papaya seedlings are liable to topple over as the result of a fungus infection. To prevent this, water the pellets with a fungicide made up according to directions on the package.

When the seedlings are a few inches high, pull out all but the sturdiest plant from each pellet. Then take a four-inch pot filled one third full with a moist average soil mix (see p. 5), and place the pellet on the soil; fill in around it and barely cover it with soil. From this point on, the plants need a lot of water and fertilizer, and should be kept in a sunny warm window. High humidity helps a great deal; a draft does not.

Habit of Growth. At its best, the papaya is a fast-growing, single-stemmed plant that grows to the size of a tree. In the tropics papayas can reach a height of ten feet in ten months and bear their first crop. Indoors the growth will be slower and there will be no fruit, but their deeply lobed maple-like leaves will add an exotic touch to any plant collection.

As Food. Delicious eaten raw.

Sugar Cane

Saccharum officinarum

GRAMINEAE

Origin. India, Indochina and the Malay Archipelago. The cultivation of sugar cane spread from India to Europe, and then to South and North America. Columbus carried sugar cane to the West Indies, from where it was brought to the United States. Today American production of sugar cane is centered mainly in the South and Hawaii.

Description. Sugar cane looks like bamboo. The canes are actually stems with nodes, or rings of root buds. At one side of the ring there is a leaf bud encased in a tiny leaf. Ask a Latin American grocer to cut off several pieces for you from the *top* part of the plant. Each piece should include two nodes.

How to Grow. Soak these "cuttings" overnight, then select a pot big enough to plant them horizontally. Fill the pot one third full with a moist average soil mix (see p. 5). Place the cuttings on the soil and cover with about two inches of more moist soil. Slip a plastic bag over the pot and put in a warm dark place.

When the cuttings sprout, remove the plastic bag and place the plant in a bright location. Roots and shoots develop from the nodes in two to three weeks.

Habit of Growth. The plant has long grasslike leaves and grows about a foot a month. For an effective display, plant half a dozen of these cuttings in a window box, which should be kept indoors in the winter.

As Food. The stalks cut into short lengths can be munched on raw or boiled. And, of course, most commercial sugar comes from sugar cane.

Tamarind

Tamarindus indica
LEGUMINOSAE

Origin. The exact origin of the tamarind tree is un-known, but the tree is thought to have come from either North Africa or Asia. Today it is cultivated throughout the tropics for its edible pods.

Description. The cinnamon-brown pods are three to eight inches long and resemble large lima bean pods. When ripe the outer shell is brittle and is easily peeled back, re-vealing the dark, sticky pulp. Each pod contains three to eight shiny brown seeds. Sometimes only the pulp is sold in plastic bags. Poke around to see if you can feel any seeds inside. These seeds are usually viable.

The seed pods are available spring and summer in Latin American grocery stores and some specialty gourmet shops.

How to Grow. Tamarinds are easily propagated from their seeds. Gently nick the hard outer shell with a sharp-edged file or piece of sandpaper and soak the seed overnight.

Plant the seeds in moistened Jiffy pellets (see p. 3). Remove enough peat from each pellet to plant one seed, and cover with the peat you removed. Put the pellets in a con-tainer that can hold water so that you can moisten it regu-larly. Slip a plastic bag over the container and give it bottom heat (see p. 8).

The seeds will germinate within two weeks, the round

seed leaves emerging atop a rather spindly stem. At this point remove the plastic bag and put the seedlings in a warm, sunny window. A few weeks later the true compound leaves will emerge. They have about nine pairs of leaflets and resemble mimosa.

When the leaves appear, transfer each pellet to a four-inch pot filled one third full with a moist average soil mix (see p. 5); place the pellets on the soil; fill in around it and barely cover it with soil. Place the pots in a sunny window—or a window with bright light will do. Keep the soil moist at all times, since a lack of water causes tamarinds to drop their leaves.

Habit of Growth. The tamarind is a large evergreen tree with lovely foliage that closes up at night and unfolds with the first light of day. The growth is slow; a well-pruned tamarind grows about a foot a year and develops a slender trunk.

Tamarinds can develop into spindly plants if they are not carefully trained. Do as follows: when there are four compound leaves on your plant, pinch out the bud in the center. This will make new branches develop within two weeks. Continue to pinch the growth centers of the new branches when they have four to six leaves. In six months you will have a lovely small tree with delicately drooping branches.

As Food. In India the pulp of the pod is used in curries and as a pickling medium for fish. In the West Indies and Latin America it is eaten fresh, baked with meat and fish or used to make a refreshing tea. Tamarinds are a mild laxative, as we learned after consuming a quart of tamarind tea on a hot spring day.

The quality of tamarinds varies enormously. Some are too acid to eat, while others have a sweet and tangy taste. You can find cans of tamarind juice in Latin American groceries.

6
Plants from Markets of the Middle and Far East

Oriental markets are among the most glorious sources of unusual fresh fruits and vegetables to grow: taro, ginger, water chestnuts, winter melon, bitter melon, litchi nuts, gingko nuts, red dates, jicama and many other fruits and nuts.

Oriental cooking has become so popular in the United States that supermarkets are springing up in Chinatowns across the country. The produce they carry is excellent, but it caters to the novice American appetite.

For really unusual goodies, go to the small shops. The merchandise is just as fresh, and much more varied. Language in these stores is a serious problem and has led to some bizarre adventures for us. Recently Debbie was on a private field trip with one of her children and spied a box of the most unusual tubers she had ever seen—oval, black and firm as a potato. Following the agreed method of purchase, she bought two for herself and two for Milly. She left the shop to the usual cries of "It won't grow, lady." (We must know that expression in six languages.)

Undaunted, she dropped the beautiful tubers off at Milly's office. Later that evening Milly called, giggling, "You bought preserved goose eggs, you idiot."

Some of our most marvelous plants have come from Oriental markets and they are well worth a little egg on the kitchen floor.

↺

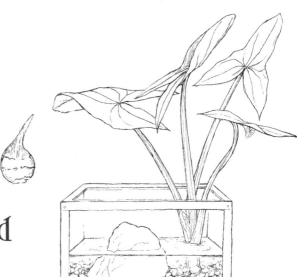

Arrowhead

Saggittaria chinensis
ALISMATACEAE

Origin. Arrowhead is an aquatic perennial native to the temperate and subtropical regions of the Orient. Highly prized for its large arrow-shaped leaves and fragrant flowers, it is often used in aquatic gardens as an ornamental plant.

Description. The plant grows from a corm that looks somewhat like a tulip bulb. Arrowhead corms are found almost year round in better Oriental markets.

How to Grow. Choose firm corms with a spike showing some growth at the top. In nature the plant grows in the rich alluvial soil of sluggish rivers and ponds. To duplicate this soil, use a rich mixture of three-fourths potting soil (from the five-and-ten) and one-fourth sand or bird gravel. Add to this a tablespoonful of fish fertilizer (available at the five-and-ten). Add water until you have the consistency of mud. The mixture will have a slight odor of low tide.

Put one inch of the mud mix in the bottom of a small empty aquarium. Place the corms on the mix and cover with two inches of sand or gravel. Add enough water so that there is a one-inch layer above the sand or gravel. Arrowheads grown this way send out stems lying on or just below the surface and rapidly form new corms. If a plant becomes too big, it can easily be cut out from its connecting plants and removed.

Habit of Growth. Arrowhead is a tall erect plant with

six- to eight-inch-wide leaves in the shape of an arrowhead. The stalks can reach a height of four feet even in the home. Flowers are white and fragrant.

As Food. Arrowhead corms are a starchy vegetable, and when cooked they have the flavor of sweet potatoes.

Bitter Melon

Momordica charantia
CUCURBITACEAE

Origin. Africa and tropical Asia. Bitter melon is a tender annual which is grown in the southern parts of the United States as an ornamental vine.

Description. You cannot mistake this unusually shaped fruit. A soft, gray-green in color, it is six to eight inches long, tapering at both ends and covered with smooth warts in longitudinal bands. As it ripens it turns a brilliant orange and makes a handsome addition to a fruit-bowl centerpiece. It is found year round in Oriental markets.

How to Grow. Remove the red aril (seed covering) from the seed—it peels off easily. Plant three seeds in a six-inch hanging-basket pot filled three quarters full with a moist average soil mix (see p. 5). Cover the seeds with a half inch of soil, then put a sheet of plastic over the top of the pot and move to a warm place. The seeds will germinate within a week. At this point, remove the plastic and place the pot in a bright or sunny window. Water frequently.

Habit of Growth. The bitter melon is a fast-growing graceful vine with deeply lobed leaves. It supports itself by means of tendrils which will wrap themselves around any support you provide. We train our vines to twine upward along the supporting thongs or wires of the hanging basket and let succeeding branches trail down.

Bitter melons are also marvelous plants to frame a window. To do this, simply provide string supports along the sides of your window. In a brightly lit window, you will soon have a beautiful natural drapery of leaves, and you will be delighted with the small yellow blooms that will appear.

You can produce your own fruit and seed by following the pollinating directions given for squash on p. 37. Although these plants are annuals, their limited life should not discourage you. They are beautiful and grow quickly and easily.

As Food. "Bitter" melon is an understatement. The fruit has a distinctive intensely bitter flavor. It is often used in soups and beef dishes and to accent bland dishes. The red aril surrounding the seed is sweet and considered a great delicacy in Chinese cooking. Avoid the seeds because they are strongly diuretic.

Chinese Dasheen (Taro)

Colocasia esculenta
ARACEAE

Origin. Asia and South Pacific. It is now commercially grown in Trinidad and sometimes called the Trinidad dasheen.

Description. The Chinese or Trinidad dasheen should not be confused with the Latin American dasheen. The Chinese corm is spherical, slightly flattened on top and pointed at the bottom. It is brown in color and has slightly darker horizontal bands circling the tuber. A good corm will be three to four inches across with incipient pink buds apparent between the horizontal stripes. In nurseries smaller corms are sold as ornamental plants (called elephant ears) at much higher prices than the ones you find year round in Chinese markets.

How to Grow. This is a plant from the tropical jungles of Asia, so it needs high humidity and warmth for germination. Put the corm in a peat moss bag (see p. 6), fold over and place in a warm dark spot. Germination can begin within three days. The top buds will begin to swell, and soon thick roots will sprout around the lower three fourths of the corm. As with all tubers, corms and bulbs, check every three or four days for any soft spots that might develop, and cut these out to prevent rot.

When the roots are three inches long, move to a pot that

is at least one inch larger in diameter than the corm. Put one or two inches of a moist average soil mix (see p. 5) in the bottom of the pot. Place the corm vertically on the soil and fill in around it, allowing one inch of the corm to show above the soil.

In its early stages of growth the corm should continue to have high humidity and bottom heat (see p. 8). After potting, place a plastic bag over the top and put the pot in a sunny window. Do not remove the plastic until the large central spike is six inches high.

Habit of Growth. Dasheen is a most dramatic performer. One of our plants attained a height of three feet within eight weeks.

Each corm develops a large cluster of exotic leaves shaped like elephant's ears (hence its common name).

As Food. Dasheens may be served boiled like potatoes or sliced and deep-fried like potato chips. In Hawaii, dasheen is known as taro, and is eaten in the form of "poi," a sticky paste made by pounding the boiled taro to a pulp.

Chinese Red Date (Jujube)

Zizyphus jujuba
RHAMNACEAE

Origin. China or possibly Syria.

Description. The Chinese red date, or jujube, has no relationship to the familiar African date palm. It is a small reddish-brown fruit the size of a kumquat and is usually sold dried and in plastic bags year round in Oriental markets. You should be able to get a hundred for under a dollar.

How to Grow. Carefully chew off all the flesh from the hard central seed. Plant one seed each in a moistened Jiffy pellet (see p. 3). Remove enough peat from each pellet to plant the rather large seed and then cover the seed with the peat you removed. Keep the pellets in a container that holds water so that they can be moistened regularly. Slip a plastic bag over the container and provide good bottom heat (see p. 8).

Germination takes ten days to three weeks. Once the first set of true leaves has appeared, place the container in a warm, sunny window or under a light unit. Older plants can withstand considerable drought, but seedlings must be kept moist.

When roots fill the Jiffy pellets it is time to transplant. For each pellet, fill a four-inch pot one third full with a moist average soil mix (see p. 5) and place the pellet on top of the soil. Fill in around it and barely cover it with moist soil.

Habit of Growth. The Chinese red date has small shiny green leaves. For an attractive bushy plant, you should pinch the stems when the plant is four inches tall, and continue to pinch succeeding branches, or else you might end up with a rather spindly plant.

The jujube tree with its small leaves and early blooming has possibilities for bonsai (a dwarfed tree shaped by pinching and pruning).

As Food. Red dates are a common fruit in China and are eaten fresh or semidried.

Ginger

Zingiber officinale
ZINGIBERACEAE

Origin. Tropical Asia, but now cultivated throughout the tropical world.

Description. Ginger is an underground stem, called a rhizome, which has buds that grow into stems and leaves. Fresh ginger is available year round at better grocery stores and ethnic markets.

How to Grow. Select a shallow, wide pot large enough to accommodate the rhizome. Fill the pot three quarters full with a moist average soil mix (see p. 5) and barely cover the rhizome with soil. Keep the soil moist and put the pot in a place that is brightly lit but not sunny. Bottom heat (see p. 8) will hasten germination.

Habit of Growth. The ginger plant grows tall quickly and looks like a stand of bamboo. In six weeks it can be three feet tall. As the old stalks die, new ones will sprout. A good ginger plant should continue to sprout for several months.

As Food. You can use the ginger in your pot by carefully slicing off about an inch from the end of the rhizome and using it in Oriental dishes.

Japanese Black Radish

Raphanus pyriformis
CRUCIFERAE

Origin. China and Japan.

Description. The Japanese black radish is a large purplish-black root that looks like a beet and ranges in width from four to ten inches. It can be found year round in Oriental grocery stores.

How to Grow. Select an attractive bowl and place a one-inch layer of pebbles in it. If the radishes are small, place two or three, root end down, directly on the pebbles. If you are using one large radish, cut off the bottom half and place the cut end on the pebbles. Add more pebbles to hold the radishes in place. Add water to the level of the pebbles and maintain this water level throughout the growing period. Place the bowl in a bright light.

Habit of Growth. This makes one of the most charming plants for a centerpiece. The large black root contrasts attractively with the glossy green leaves which sprout within a few days. The leaves die back in about six weeks, and then appears a lovely bluish-white six-inch spike of bloom.

As Food. This vegetable is milder than the conventional garden radish. It is usually grated into an Oriental dipping sauce or cooked with Chinese vegetables.

Japanese White Radish

Raphanus longipinalus
CRUCIFERAE

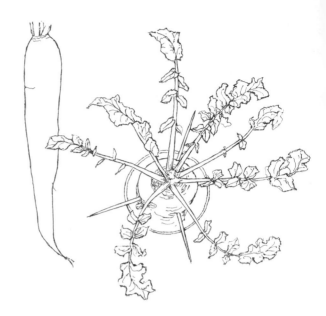

Origin. China and Japan.

Description. A long dull-white root some eight to twelve inches in length and two to three inches across, the white radish can reach a size of twenty pounds. It is found year round in Oriental markets.

How to Grow. Jars large enough to accommodate this root are hard to find, so cut it in half to fit whatever is available. Stick three toothpicks into the skin of the root about one third of the way down from the top. Fill the jar with water and allow the toothpicks to rest on the rim of the jar. Keep adding water to replenish the water that evaporates.

Habit of Growth. The white radish produces lovely lush foliage with leaves ten to eighteen inches high which appear within two weeks. We have never gotten this particular root to bloom, but its long, curled foliage more than makes up for this deficiency.

As Food. This plant is milder than the common garden radish and is used in Oriental cooking, chiefly for dips or as an ingredient in mixed vegetables.

Jicama
Exogonium bracteatum
CONVOLVULACEAE

Origin. Tropical America.

Description. The jicama, a member of the morning glory family, is a vine whose root looks like a large, dusty-brown top. The roots vary greatly in size, from four to eight inches across. Strangely enough, although they are cultivated in Latin America, we have been unable to find them anywhere but in Oriental markets, usually from spring through early fall.

How to Grow. Place the pointed end of a root in a glass or jar of water just big enough to support it, with the bottom two inches of the root immersed in water. Place in a warm spot in the home.

Within one to two weeks white bumps will appear all over the bottom—these will be roots. Stems will not begin to sprout until a healthy root system has developed, a process which may take a month or more. During this time the jicama will shrink perceptibly in size. Once the glass is filled with roots it is time to transplant. Fill an eight-inch pot one third full with a moist average soil mix (see p. 5). Place the root on the soil and fill in around it, allowing the top inch of the root to show above the surface. Place the pot in a bright sunny window.

Habit of Growth. In about six to eight weeks, fuzzy

leafless stems will develop. Do not be discouraged—the plant needs about two months to become a lovely leafy trailing plant.

As Food. Jicamas taste somewhat like sweet potatoes and are prepared the same way.

Litchi

Litchi chinensis
SAPINDACEAE

Origin. Southern China. The litchi tree has been cultivated in China for over two thousand years.

Description. Dried litchi nuts can be bought every day of the year in Chinese groceries but these will not grow. Fresh litchi nuts that can be planted are found in those stores only during the summer months. They are round, rosy-red fruits with little bumps on them.

How to Grow. Remove the skin and eat the delicious pulp. The seed must be planted within five days after being taken from the fruit.

Plant the seeds in moistened Jiffy pellets (see p. 3). Remove enough peat from each pellet to plant one seed, and cover it with the peat you removed. Put the pellets in a dish that can hold water so that you can moisten them regularly. Slip a plastic bag over the container and place the container where it will have bottom heat (see p. 8). The seeds should sprout in about two weeks.

Allow the seedlings to grow in the pellets until roots fill the bottom of the pellets. At this point transfer each pellet to a four-inch flower pot. Fill it one third full with a moist average soil mix (see p. 5). Place the pellet on the soil, fill in around it, and barely cover it with soil. Place the pots in a bright window. To transplant to larger pots, see p. 9.

Habit of Growth. Outdoors the litchi tree grows to a height of forty feet. We had one indoors that grew to a height of six feet in about three years. It is a beautiful plant with delicate shiny leaves.

As Food. Fresh litchi nuts are delicious and quite unlike the more familiar dried litchis.

Persimmon

Diospyros kaki
EBENACEAE

Origin. China. Brought to Japan at an early date, persimmons are the chief fruit product of that country today. They were introduced to the United States from Japan by the Perry Expedition, and are now grown in California and the South.

Description. Although most persimmons are seedless, our experience has been that the smaller varieties are more likely to bear seeds. The seeds are dark brown, oblong and at least a half inch long. Do not be misled by the tiny black seeds found in the tip of the fruit—these are abortive seeds and will not grow.

Persimmons are so delicious that it is not difficult to eat your way through a dozen or so to find a few seeds.

The fruits are available in late fall and early winter in all kinds of markets.

How to Grow. We recommend stratifying the seeds in the refrigerator (see p. 8). We have tried planting them directly into Jiffy pellets without the cold treatment; the seeds germinated rapidly (two to three weeks) but their subsequent growth was stunted, and the majority died. In contrast, those we stratified gave us 100 percent germination and became sturdy little trees.

After removing the seeds from the refrigerator, plant one

seed per moistened Jiffy pellet (see p. 3). Remove enough of the moist peat to plant the seed, and cover the seed with the peat you removed. Put the pellets in a container that can hold water so that you can moisten them regularly. Slip a plastic bag over the container and give good bottom heat (see p. 8). Germination takes about two to three weeks. Once the seedlings have sprouted remove the plastic bag and put the container in a bright window.

When the plants are three inches high, transfer each pellet to a four-inch pot filled one third full with a moist average soil mix (see p. 5); place the pellet on the soil and

Habit of Growth. Young seedlings are ugly ducklings. First the stem appears, shaped like a loop, but within two weeks it should straighten out and the first leaves appear. These leaves are shiny and pointed and bear no resemblance to the heavily veined mature leaves which develop within a month.

When a plant reaches a foot in height, pinch it back to emphasize its naturally rounded shape. Persimmon plants will grow best in a southern or western window; they must be carefully watered and not allowed to dry out. Grown indoors, the plants will not flower.

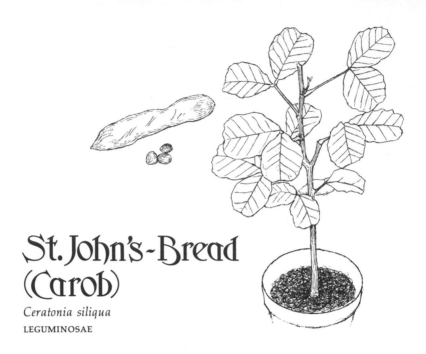

St. John's-Bread (Carob)

Ceratonia siliqua
LEGUMINOSAE

Origin. Mediterranean region. St. John's-bread is a stately tree whose dried pods have been found in the ruins of Pompeii. When John the Baptist wandered in the desert, the "wild honey" he was said to have eaten could have been the pulp of these pods. The uniform seeds are supposed to have been used in former times by goldsmiths to check the carat weight of gold.

The pods are found year round in gourmet shops and Near Eastern markets.

Description. The pods look something like large lima bean pods that have turned brown. Inside are hard, shiny seeds.

How to Grow. Remove the seeds from the pod. Nick each seed with a sharp-edged file or a piece of sandpaper and soak for one or two days. When the seeds swell, they are ready to plant.

Take a moistened Jiffy pellet (see p. 3), remove a little of the peat, plant one seed and cover it with the peat you removed. Plant at least three seeds, one to a pellet. Keep the pellets in a container that can hold water so that you can moisten the pellets regularly. Slip a plastic bag over the container and put it where it will have bottom heat (see p. 8). The seeds should sprout within a week. When the seedlings show, remove the plastic bag and put the container in a sunny window.

The seedlings should be transplanted into four-inch pots when they are six inches tall. Fill each pot one third full with a moist average soil mix (see p. 5). Place a pellet on the soil, fill in around it and barely cover it with soil. Place the pots in a bright sunny window and keep the soil moist but not soggy.

Habit of Growth. The leaves of St. John's-bread are oval, shiny and the color of bronze, and the stem turns woody in its early stages. St. John's-bread trees are slow-growing and flourish in an arid climate.

As Food. The pods have a rather mocha-like taste and the gummy texture is rather pleasant. Beware of crunching down on a seed—it's a good way to chip a tooth.

Frankly, we have wondered who actually eats these pods. Most of our texts refer to them as fodder, and as food for human consumption only in times of famine. Yet we bought them at one of the most expensive gourmet shops in New York. We asked the clerks to ask other customers what they did with them. After a summer of research, all they could tell us was that several elderly ladies with heavy European accents were buying them for heart and gall bladder conditions. Not much help.

Water Chestnut

Eleocharis tuberosa
CYPERACEAE

Origin. China.

Description. A round, dark-brown corm one inch across and about one inch high, the water chestnut is flat on the bottom with one or two small horns or spikes on the top. It is found year round in Chinese markets.

How to Grow. Water chestnuts are aquatic plants which are quite difficult to germinate. Select only the firmest, freshest corms. Place two or three in a pint jar filled with tepid water, cover and place the jar in a warm dark place. Change the water every three days and check the corms for soft spots; if these develop on any of the corms discard them entirely.

In three to six weeks white spikes will appear at the top of the corms. When the spikes are about two inches long, the plants are ready to be transferred to four-inch pots, each filled with a mixture of three-fourths potting-soil (from the five-and-ten) and one-fourth sand or bird gravel. Add one drop of fish fertilizer (also available at the five-and-ten) to each pot, and water until you have the consistency of mud.

Plant the corms up to the base of the spikes and cover the soil with a thin layer of pebbles, which will help hold the soil in place. Immerse the pots in a large glass dish containing at least six inches of water. Place in a warm, sunny window.

You will have to freshen the water at least once a week to

prevent stagnation and supply aeration. To do this, place the glass container under a *gentle* stream of water and let the water overflow for a few minutes. What dirt rises to the top will settle, but be careful not to expose the corms. It will be necessary to add more soil to your pots from time to time.

Habit of Growth. The water chestnut is not a beautiful plant. You will soon find you are growing a jugful of grass with no hope of a harvest. However, it is a rapid grower and in the proper container it could be an interesting conversation piece.

As Food. The peeled corms have the texture of a radish and are very sweet. Water chestnuts make a wonderful addition to meat and vegetable dishes.

7
Exotica

$\mathcal{M}$ ost of the fruits in this section are rare—a challenge both to the palate and to your horticultural ability. All are cultivated in this country, but some are not commercially distributed and others have a very limited season.

Some names are unfamiliar: black sapote, Chinese star apple, kiwi, cherimoya, sapodilla. But do not be put off by their strange names and shapes. Wonderful gardening and adventurous eating await you.

One hot day in Miami we were served a high tea of cherimoya shake served with a slice of chilled mango on pound cake. We doubt any tea was ever so refreshing. Our hosts gave us the seeds, and within two weeks we had mango and cherimoya seedlings.

You may come across many of these fruits in your travels to tropical vacation resorts. *Do not smuggle;* there are easy and legitimate ways to import seeds. Friends of ours who tried the illegal way have had disastrous experiences. One smuggled prickly pear in wet bathing trunks and got through customs without any trouble, but the next time he put on the trunks he found himself covered with tiny spines that took weeks to come out. Another smuggled some sapodilla (a source of the chicle in chewing gum) and spent an hour in the bathtub soaking before she could remove the fruit from herself.

Black Sapote

Diospyros ebenaster
EBENACEAE

Origin. Mexico and Central America. Black sapote is believed to have been cultivated by the Indians since 4000 B.C. Today it is commercially grown for its wood, ebony.

Description. The name is confusing because this fruit is neither black on the outside nor a member of the sapote family. The flesh, however, is black when ripe and looks like axle grease. When you buy the fruit in the store (available off and on throughout the year in the South and occasionally in ethnic markets elsewhere), it looks like a small green persimmon. Within the dark pulpy mass there are six large brown seeds about a half inch long and a half inch wide.

How to Grow. The seeds germinate rapidly in ten days to three weeks, and germination is close to 100 percent.

Plant the seeds in moistened Jiffy pellets (see p. 3): Remove enough peat from each pellet to plant one seed, and cover with the peat you removed. Put the pellets in a dish that can hold water so that you can moisten them regularly. Slip a plastic bag over the container and give it bottom heat (see p. 8).

When the seedlings emerge from the soil the stems look like brown loops, but soon the stems will straighten out and the leaves will appear. At this point remove the plastic bag and put the seedlings in a sunny window.

When the seedlings have their second set of leaves, it is

time to transplant them into four-inch pots, each filled one third full with a moist average soil mix (see p. 5). Place the pellets on the soil, fill in around them, and barely cover them. Place the pots in a sunny window and keep the soil moist at all times.

Habit of Growth. The most outstanding feature of the young black sapote is its hard black trunk, which forms almost before the second set of leaves does. The new leaves are a dark glossy green, oblong and slightly pointed, and they contrast handsomely with the dark bark.

Growth is relatively slow, less than a foot a year. Older plants should be transplanted to six-inch pots when the roots show through the bottom (see p. 9).

As Food. The black sapote is frequently referred to as the chocolate pudding tree because of the color of the flesh and the hint of chocolate in its flavor. When the fruit is fully ripe (the test is that it feels almost rotten to the touch), try mixing it with a little sour cream and crème de cacao and serving it as a sauce or pudding. Or you can follow baking recipes for persimmon puddings and cakes and again have the same delicious chocolate taste.

Cherimoya

Annona cherimola
ANNONACEAE

Origin. Tropical America. The cherimoya may well be the oldest cultivated fruit in the New World; pottery urns in the shape of cherimoyas have been unearthed from ancient burial grounds in Peru. Today cherimoyas are grown throughout the tropical world. In the United States they are grown in California.

Description. The cherimoya is available in the winter in gourmet shops. They may cost as much as two dollars a fruit, but they are worth it. The heart-shaped gray-green fruit can range in size from eight ounces to six pounds. About twenty-five black seeds, three quarters of an inch long and pointed at one end, are buried in the creamy-white flesh of the fruit.

How to Grow. The seeds may be started in moistened Jiffy pellets (see p. 3). With your fingers, remove enough peat from each pellet so that you can press a seed (pointed end down) into the peat. Cover with the peat you removed. Place the pellets in a container to which you can add water to keep them constantly moist. Slip a plastic bag over the container and place it where it can have bottom heat (see p. 8).

Seeds will sprout in one to three weeks. You can expect 95 percent germination, so plant only as many as you think you want. Dry unused seeds overnight and place them in an airtight container. They will retain their vitality for several years.

When the seedlings show, remove the plastic bag and put the container in a bright window or under lights (see p. 10).

When roots fill the pellets, transfer each pellet to a four-inch flower pot filled one third full with a moist average soil mix (see p. 5): Place the pellet on the soil, fill in around it and barely cover it. Place the pots in a bright window or under lights. When the plants grow too big for their pots (roots come through the hole in the bottom), move them to six-inch pots, following the directions on p. 9.

Habit of Growth. When a seedling emerges, it is looped over like a swan with its head in the water. Soon the seed pod appears on a three-inch neck and just sits there for several weeks while the leaves slowly develop one by one. It is not unusual to see a seedling with six fully developed pale-green leaves and the seed pod still on the plant. It is a temptation to remove the silly-looking seed pod, but leave it alone.

The tree will grow about eight inches a year but will not bear fruit. It has a gently curving stem which needs to be pinched to become more branched and compact in shape. Some kinds of cherimoya are deciduous, that is, they drop their leaves. Should your plant shed its leaves in the late fall, just water it less. It will leaf out again after this dormant period.

The cherimoya tree has a graceful quality that makes it an indoor plant to be treasured.

As Food. Cherimoya is the queen of the tropical fruits of the New World. Its texture is like that of custard and its flavor a combination of strawberry, pineapple, banana and yogurt. It makes a delicious dessert fruit, as well as a soothing refreshing drink. If you lace the drink with brandy, you have dessert and cordial all in one.

Chinese Star Apple

Averrhoa camrambola
OXALIDACEAE

Origin. East Indies and China.

Description. The Chinese star apple is a stunning addition to any fruit-bowl display. It is ovoid, golden-yellow, and has several prominent ribs. Despite its name, it is not available in Chinese markets, but is found in better grocery stores throughout late spring to early winter.

How to Grow. Carefully remove the seeds, which are deep within the fruit, and plant them in Jiffy pellets (see p. 3). Moisten the pellets and remove enough peat from each pellet to plant one seed, covering it with the peat you removed. Put the pellets in a dish to which you can add water to moisten them regularly. Slip a plastic bag over the container and give them good bottom heat (see p. 8). The seeds should germinate within three weeks. When the first set of leaves emerges, remove the plastic bag and place the seedlings in a bright draft-free window.

When roots fill the pellets or the seedlings are three to four inches tall, it is time to transplant them. For each pellet, fill a four-inch pot one third full with a moist average soil mix (see p. 5). Place the pellet on the soil and fill in around it, just barely covering it. Place the pots in a bright draft-free window.

Habit of Growth. The Chinese star apple grows slowly,

about a foot a year, and will not bear fruit indoors. Each leaf has seven to eleven heart-shaped leaflets which give the plant a feathery appearance not unlike that of mimosa. At night the leaves close up. This is one of the most graceful and charming plants in our collection.

As Food. These fruits vary greatly in quality. At their best, they are like a cross between a sweet grapefruit and an orange. At their worst, they are very sour and full of tannic acid. The quality can be judged by smelling the fruit: if it has a sweet aroma, chances are that it will be sweet. Chinese star apples can be eaten plain or as a substitute for grapefruit in an avocado and grapefruit salad. In general they make a wonderful addition to any fruit cup or salad. Sour varieties are often used for jams and jellies.

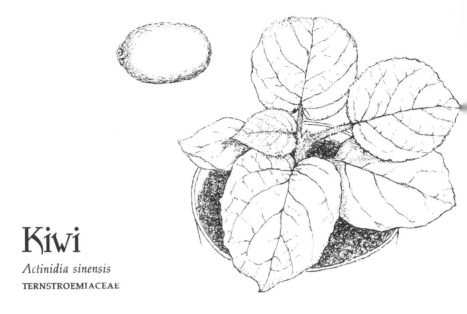

Kiwi

Actinidia sinensis
TERNSTROEMIACEAE

Origin. China. The kiwi in our markets today are all grown in New Zealand. For some unknown reason the fruit has the same name as the flightless kiwi bird of New Zealand.

Description. The fruit has the shape of a large gooseberry and is brown and hairy with an almost woody texture to its thin skin; the flesh is a beautiful translucent green. It can be purchased in early summer and fall in good urban and suburban supermarkets.

How to Grow. When you slice the fruit you will notice hundreds of tiny black seeds. Scoop out a few and remove all traces of flesh by rolling them on a paper towel with your fingers.

Next fill a small plastic container with moist peat moss and scatter the seeds on the surface. Cover lightly with more moist peat. Slip a plastic bag over the container and put the container in the refrigerator, leaving it there for four to six weeks.

When you remove the seeds from their mock winter, put the container in a warm spot. The seedlings should sprout shortly thereafter. When they do, remove the plastic bag and put the container in a bright window.

When the seedlings are two inches high, transplant them. Gently loosen the soil under each seedling with a pencil and lift the young plant out by the leaves. Fill a four-inch pot with an average soil mix (see p. 5). Use the pencil to make a hole deep enough to receive the roots, and cover about an inch of the stem with soil. Water well and place the pot in a bright window.

Habit of Growth. In nature the kiwi is a deciduous vine attaining a length of twenty-five feet. Indoors its size is easily controlled by judicious pruning and by limiting the size of the pot.

The kiwi grows about three feet a year. It is a beautiful plant with soft, fuzzy, pale-green leaves. Young seedlings should be staked, and older plants should be given supports on which to twine. It helps to attach the plant to its support with "twist-ems."

As Food. The kiwi is a delicious breakfast or dessert fruit. Its flavor is reminiscent of strawberries and watermelon. It also makes an unusual addition to a fruit compote.

Loquat

Eriobotrya japonica
ROSACEAE

Origin. China and Japan. Today the loquat is much cultivated throughout the subtropical regions of the world; in the United States it is grown commercially in the Gulf region, where it is known as Japanese plum.

Description. The fruit is pale yellow to light orange with smooth, thin skin. Each fruit is small (one to two inches), round, and sold in clusters much as kumquats are. It bruises easily, but the brown spots are not an indication of age or inferior fruit. Loquats can be purchased in late spring and early summer in gourmet markets.

How to Grow. Each fruit will have one to three large seeds in the central cavity. Wash off any residue of flesh and plant the seeds in moistened Jiffy pellets (see p. 3). Remove enough peat from each pellet to plant one seed, and cover it with the peat you removed. Put the pellets in a dish that can hold water so that they can be kept constantly moist. Slip a plastic bag over the container and place it where it will have bottom heat (see p. 8).

The seeds should germinate in two to four weeks. When they do, remove the plastic bag and place the container in a bright warm place, avoiding direct sunlight and drafts. A bright north window is good—or a bright place in an indoor light garden. When roots fill the pellets, transfer each pellet to a four-inch flower pot filled one third full with a moist average soil mix (see p. 5); place the pellet on the soil, fill in around it, and barely cover it with soil. Put the pots back in a north window or under fluorescent lights.

To advance to larger pots, see p. 9.

Habit of Growth. The loquat is a lovely symmetrical evergreen tree. The new leaves are an attractive woolly gray at first and then they change to a dark glossy green. The leaves can be as large as eight inches on a mature plant; on young trees they are four to five inches long.

Most loquats will begin to branch at the end of the first year, by which time the plant should be eight to ten inches tall. If yours does not branch, pinch the center growing tip and within a few weeks new branches will form. In its first few years the plant grows slowly, but later it may grow up to two feet a year.

As Food. Loquats are delicious fresh. Their flavor is like that of a peach or nectarine. The fruit is also used in jams and jellies and canned as a dessert fruit.

Pomegranate

Punica granatum
PUNICACEAE

Origin. Southern Asia. It is now naturalized throughout the Mediterranean and in the southern United States.

Description. The pomegranate is a red spherical· fruit ranging in size from three to six inches; its skin is thick and leathery. The fruit is found in the fall in good urban and suburban supermarkets.

How to Grow. Cut the fruit open and you will find lots of seeds, each inside a large red juicy aril (seed covering). Put on an apron and have plenty of paper towels handy. Roll the seeds gently on several thicknesses of paper towels. The red juice of the arils will squirt all over the place, but don't worry—it doesn't stain. Once the arils are removed, place the seeds on a clean towel to dry. You may plant them directly, but if you wish to store them, let the seeds dry for twenty-four hours and put them in an airtight jar, where they will retain their vitality for at least a year.

Plant the seeds in moist Jiffy pellets (see p. 3). With your fingers remove enough peat from each pellet so that you can press a few seeds into the peat and cover them up with the peat you removed. Place the pellets in a dish to which you can add water to moisten them regularly. Slip a plastic bag over the container and give it good bottom heat (see p. 8). With proper heat, the seeds should germinate within five to ten days. If you cannot supply bottom heat, the seeds may take more than a month to sprout.

Once they have sprouted, remove the plastic bag and place the seedlings in a warm sunny location. Keep moist at all times. When the seedlings are three to four inches high or when their roots fill the pellets, it is time to transplant. For each pellet, fill a four-inch pot one third full with a moist average soil mix (see p. 5). Place the pellet on the soil, fill in around it and barely cover it. If you are using a fluorescent light unit, this is a good plant to grow in it. Otherwise a windowsill with southern or western exposure is best.

Pomegranates are ideal plants for the average American home, which tends to lack humidity. Once past the seedling stage, they do not require the humidity necessary for growing tropical plants. When the plant is actively growing, keep the soil moist, but in the fall it should be kept on the dry side.

Habit of Growth. In nature pomegranates can attain a height of ten to fifteen feet. When they are grown in the home, their size is easily controlled by pinching off the top buds. Pinching also prevents the plant from becoming spindly. So when the first true six leaves appear, pinch back to four leaves. Soon new branches will emerge. Pinch the branches as soon as they have six new leaves and keep pinching until you have the shape you want. The dainty leaves and woody trunk of the pomegranate make it an ideal subject for bonsai (decorative dwarfed trees).

As Food. Pomegranates are delicious as a dessert fruit, albeit a little messy, and their juice is the main component of grenadine syrup. Mohammed once said, "To eat the pomegranate is to purge oneself of enemies and hate."

Prickly Pear

Opuntia ficus indica
CACTACEAE

Origin. Central and South America. It is generally thought that the fruit was introduced to the Old World by Columbus. Today it is extensively cultivated in North Africa and Sicily, and in the United States it is grown in the Southwest.

Description. The fruit is brick-red in color and is about the size of a large hen's egg. When picked fresh, it is covered with minute spines, but those sold commercially have had most of these removed. The flesh is a deep pink with many small black seeds. The fruit is found in the fall and early winter in gourmet shops and some supermarkets.

How to Grow. Scoop out a dozen or more seeds and wash off any flesh clinging to them. Plant them immediately in a flat (a shallow box), using a soilless mix (see p. 5). The seeds are small and need only to be dusted with a thin layer of mix. Cover the flat with plastic and give good bottom heat (see p. 8).

Germination is erratic. Our first seeds sprouted within ten days, but others in the same flat did not sprout for another two months. Do not discard the flat after a few seeds have germinated. Many more will be on the way.

Once the first seedlings have sprouted, move the flat to a warm, sunny place or a light unit. Keep it covered with plastic until a good proportion of the seeds have germinated. Seedlings require careful watering. Do not allow the seed bed to dry out.

When the seedlings are an inch high and a distinctive spiny leaf has developed on each, they may be transplanted into one-inch pots. Gently loosen the soil under each seedling with a pencil and lift it out by the leaves. For each seedling, fill a pot with a moist average soil mix (see p. 5) and, with the pencil, make a hole deep enough to receive the roots, and cover about a quarter inch of the stem with soil.

When roots fill the pots, transplant to four-inch pots (see p. 9).

Habit of Growth. Young plants bear no resemblance to the mature ones and you may well wonder what has sprouted in your seed bed. At first two fleshy spineless leaves appear. Within two weeks, you will notice tiny green bristles developing between the leaves. These are the beginnings of the first true leaves, which in this case are fleshy pads.

The prickly pear grows slowly, developing at the rate of one pad every six months. It is most attractive when small.

In nature the prickly pear can grow to be fifteen feet tall. Grown indoors it will not bear fruit.

As Food. Prickly pears combine the delicious flavors of the watermelon and the strawberry. To serve, simply cut them horizontally.

Sapodilla

Achras zapota
SAPOTACEAE

Origin. Tropical America, probably southern Mexico. Sapodilla trees have been found growing wild throughout the West Indies and Central America. The fruit is the chief source of chicle, which is the base for chewing gum.

Description. Sapodillas are sold under many different names, including chicle, naseberry, sapote (not to be confused with black sapote). The fruit is easily recognizable. It is round to slightly oblong, and about the size of a small apple. The rusty-brown skin has a thin woody texture, and the flesh when ripe is a pale golden brown. Each fruit has five to eight seeds, each about half an inch long.

How to Grow. The seeds germinate easily. Remove a little of the peat from a moistened Jiffy pellet (see p. 3) and place each seed, pointed end down, on the pellet and cover it with the peat you removed. Keep the pellets in a container that can hold water so that you can moisten them regularly. Slip a plastic bag over the container and put it where it has bottom heat (see p. 8).

Germination takes ten days to three weeks and is just about 100 percent.

When the seeds sprout, remove the plastic bag and put the container in a bright window or under lights. Keep the pellets moist.

When roots fill the pellets, transfer them to four-inch pots, each filled one third full with a moist average soil mix (see p. 5). Place each pellet on the soil, fill in around it and barely cover it. Place the pots where they will get bright light but not direct sunlight. The soil should be kept slightly moist at all times.

Habit of Growth. In their native habitat, sapodillas are evergreen trees which can attain a height of thirty to forty feet. In your home a tree will grow about six inches a year and be compact and erect. Natural branching should occur in the second year, but if it doesn't, pinch the central bud. The foliage is attractive, the leaves being a dark glossy green on top and pale green beneath. These leaves are about three to four inches long and have a leathery texture. Early in the first year the plant develops an attractive cinnamon-colored bark. Grown indoors, the plant will not bear fruit.

As Food. Sapodillas are a dessert fruit which when properly ripened feel almost rotten to the touch. The flavor and texture at this stage are similar to those of a pear, but much sweeter. We serve them with a slice of lemon or lime.

No fruit varies so much in quality during its different stages of ripening as does the sapodilla. When firm and unripe, one bite can pucker the mouth for an hour. In the middle stages sapodillas taste like good old-fashioned sour apples. We once made a disastrous mistake by trying to make an "apple" pie with them at that stage. The chicle in the pulp turned it into a rubber pie.

Spanish Lime (Genip)

Melicocca bijuga
SAPINDACEAE

Origin. Northern South America, Central America and the West Indies. Today Spanish lime is grown commercially in southern Florida and southern California.

The name is deceptive. The fruit bears no resemblance to a lime in texture, taste or appearance, and it is not a member of the Citrus family.

Description. Spanish limes are sold in twiggy, rather unattractive clusters. The individual fruit is round and about one inch in diameter with gray-green skin that makes it look like a leathery-textured grape. It splits open easily, revealing cream-colored translucent flesh surrounding one large seed the size of a peanut. Spanish limes are sold under several different names, such as genipe, knepe and queenpea. We have found them in the spring in Japanese, Chinese and Spanish markets.

How to Grow. Carefully chew the sweet flesh from the seed. Plant one seed per Jiffy pellet (see p. 3): with your fingers remove enough of the peat from a moistened pellet to accommodate the seed, and cover the seed with the peat you just removed. Place the pellets in a dish to which you can add water to moisten them regularly. Slip a plastic bag over the container and give them good bottom heat (see p. 8).

The seeds germinate rapidly in ten days to two weeks.

When the first leaves appear, remove the plastic bag and transfer the seedlings to a warm bright spot. The seedlings should be given as much humidity as possible and never allowed to dry out.

When the seedlings are three or four inches high or when their roots have filled the pellets, it is time to transplant. For each seedling, take a four-inch pot and fill it one third full with a moist average soil mix (see p. 5); place the pellet on the soil, fill in around it and barely cover it. Return the pots to a warm bright window.

Habit of Growth. Spanish limes grow about ten to twelve inches a year. The plant is most noteworthy for its very unusual light-green foliage. It has several large ruffled leaflets that rise from a six- to eight-inch leaf stalk. The plant's shape is so compact that pinching and pruning are not really necessary to achieve a well-shaped plant.

As Food. The fruits are eaten fresh. The flesh, which is slightly fibrous, has a flavor that is a cross between those of a grape and a mango.

In Cuba cowboys carried bunches of Spanish limes on their saddlehorns to quench their thirst. And indeed they are very refreshing on a hot day.

When roasted like chestnuts, the seeds taste very much like peanuts.

About the Authors

MILLICENT SELSAM is the author and editor of numerous award-winning children's books on the natural sciences, including *Biography of an Atom,* written with J. Bronowski, which won the Thomas A. Edison Award. She received her M.A. in biology from Columbia University and has taught biology at Brooklyn College and in New York City high schools. She is a native of New York.

DEBORAH PETERSON has lectured for the past eight years throughout the Northeast on growing plants from fruits and seeds. She is a frequent speaker for the New York Horticultural Society and for the New York Indoor Light Gardening Society, of which she is an officer. She lives with her family in New York City.